FAMILY OF FAITH
LIBRARY

Family of Faith Library

W9-BIF-560

Substitute Teacher
HANDBOOK

Expectations, Classroom Management, and Fill-in Activities
Second Edition

© **Substitute Teacher Training Institute**
8200 University Blvd.
Logan, UT 84322-8200
(800) 922-4693
(801) 797-3182
subed@cc.usu.edu
ISBN: 1-890563-03-X

Utah State
UNIVERSITY

SECONDARY 9–12

What It's All About!

*"Education is not the filling of a pail,
but the lighting of a fire."*

William Butler Yeats

In every state, district and school in America, an estimated 8% of all the children attending school are being taught by substitute teachers each day. Depending upon whether one looks at this as an opportunity or a problem, will greatly affect the quality of the teaching during this time.

The Substitute Teacher Training Institute at Utah State University and many districts across the country see substitute teaching as an opportunity to give students experiences that would be difficult for permanent teachers to provide. You, the substitute teacher, are the key player in making this a success.

During the course of researching and assembling the material for this handbook hundreds of surveys were completed by both permanent teachers and substitute teachers. There were many positive and exciting results shared by these teachers across the country. This handbook will highlight these tools, techniques, and skills, showing you how to incorporate them into your teaching.

Permanent teachers are very possessive, as you would be if someone came into your kitchen or shop, taking over while you were away. Since permanent teachers want the best for their students, 70% of them spend more than 45 minutes preparing lesson plans for the substitute teacher. These same teachers, however, say that their best substitute teachers are those who have their own "bag of tricks" and use fill-in activities when appropriate. No one would ask a right-handed backup quarterback to throw left-handed just because the main quarterback is left-handed, nor would anyone enjoy listening to a substitute speaker read a speech that had been written by someone else. So let me tell you a quick story . . .

My own father became a world-renowned chemistry professor at a major U.S. university, making significant contributions to America's space and science programs. What few people know is that he was turned on to chemistry when he was in the 7th grade. The school principal, working as a substitute teacher one day, showed the class how to produce hydrogen from dilute hydrochloric acid and zinc instead of entertaining the students with games. This simple but impressive demonstration was a pivotal moment in my father's life. He made chemistry his career, all because a substitute teacher understood his role was that of a teacher, not a baby-sitter!

If *"Education is not the filling of a pail, but the lighting of a fire,"* trained substitute teachers can light that same type of fire over and over again from classroom to classroom. By implementing the helpful hints from teachers, classroom management techniques and fill-in activities, you will enjoy substitute teaching as well as provide great benefits to students, teachers, administrators, and parents.

Geoffrey G. Smith
Executive Director

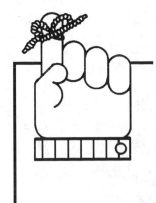

Remember

The information in this handbook is not intended to replace the rules and regulations of your local district. Use only those suggestions and activities from this handbook that do not conflict with your district's policies.

© Substitute Teacher Training Institute

Acknowledgments

Geoffrey G. Smith

Mr. Smith is currently the Executive Director of the Substitute Teacher Training Institute (STTI) at Utah State University (USU). Mr. Smith has been involved in teacher inservice and water education as Manager of the International Office for Water Education also at USU.

Cynthia Murdock

Cynthia Murdock is the curriculum director of STTI. Her teacher-leader ability along with experience as a substitute and permanent teacher has given her an excellent background to develop ideas and materials for STTI. In addition to developing curriculum, Cynthia is a workshop instructor and edits the *SubExchange* newsletter. She enjoys collecting children's books, writing, and teaching.

Sara Hacken

Sara Hacken is an award-winning teacher who has prepared workshops at the local, state, and national level. She has written a wide variety of curriculum materials stemming from her interest in diverse topics such as electronics, architecture, child labor law, chemistry, art, history, and inventions. Mrs. Hacken worked for two years as a substitute teacher while she was earning her elementary teaching credentials. She has been teaching and writing curriculum for eleven years.

Carolyn Goodwin Schubach

For the past five years, Ms. Schubach has been a principal in the Murray City School District. She is also the President of Utah ASCD (Association of Supervision and Curriculum Development) and Director Elect Utah Principals Academy. Ms. Schubach has taught workshops in classroom management, cooperative learning and curriculum integration in both district and university settings.

Donald R. Daugs

Professor Daugs is recognized nationally as a leader in science teaching methodology and science, technology and society. He presents papers on science teaching methodology regularly at one or more national and international conferences annually. He has authored numerous publications including *The Comprehensive Water Education Book, Sodia Science, A User's Manual for Science Teaching Methods* and *Holding an Invention Fair Science and Math Events: Connecting and Competing.*

Diane Iverson

Mrs. Iverson received her teaching degree at University of Missouri, and has been substitute teaching for 8 years. Last year alone, she taught every day of the school year as a substitute teacher. She has been involved with writing and compiling curriculum for substitute teachers in several states and is currently a permanent teacher.

Thanks also to: Rosemary Tolman, Betty Hansen, Larry Mortensen, and Candy Wilke.

© Substitute Teacher Training Institute

Table of Contents

© Substitute Teacher Training Institute

Chapter 1

Expectations and Suggestions

Congratulations! You've decided to become a substitute teacher. Your family and friends have probably offered their support for this new venture. Typically cheery responses might include:

"The Army/Navy store still has a few steel-tipped combat boots available. You'll be able to have your own pair — believe me, you'll need them," or "I'm sorry. I knew you had some financial setbacks, but I didn't know things were this serious."

As you might have gathered, the implication here is that you are really desperate.

However, as many of us know, substitute teaching is not an act committed out of desperation. Substitute teaching is an important service in our schools. It is a rare teacher who never gets sick or is never out of the classroom. Principals and teachers value a good substitute teacher. Preparing suitable materials for a substitute teacher is not always easy or convenient. The ideas in this book are designed to help you handle challenging situations when the materials left are inadequate.

Regardless of whether or not you are a certified teacher, you can still become an expert in substitute teaching by focusing on new techniques, ideas, activities, and suggestions. With these skills in your repertoire, you will be in such demand that you will be scheduling your substitute teaching assignments weeks in advance, students will see you in the hall and ask when you are coming to their class, and parents will be calling the district requesting they hire you full-time.

This handbook presents ways to reduce your learning curve if you are just beginning substitute teaching and gives interesting new ideas for your classes if you have been teaching for a while. This chapter involves learning from others, whether from permanent teachers, substitute teachers or from districts. Quotes are taken from comments gathered from hundreds of survey forms completed by permanent teachers, substitute teachers, and administrators.

Expectations:

Both administrators and permanent teachers appreciate having a substitute teacher who arrives early, follows lesson plans, and has good leadership skills. An ideal substitute is creative in presenting new material to the class, knows how to handle behavior problems, and tries to utilize the regular procedures of the permanent teacher whenever possible. Since every teacher is unique and has different expectations, a substitute teacher needs to be versatile. There are a number of basic expectations that need to be met regardless of the assignment.

Expectations from Permanent Teachers
- Classroom Management
- Following the Lesson Plans
- Pulling from your "Bag of Tricks" (when appropriate)
- Professionalism
- Leaving a Report for the Permanent Teacher

Classroom Management

Teachers hope that whoever takes over in their absence, will be capable of having the same kind of order and discipline which they themselves maintain daily. Sometimes they forget, however, that this is nearly impossible for someone who doesn't even know the students' names. Permanent teachers have the first few weeks of each school year to establish routines that work. This handbook provides you with the necessary tools to bring your own routines to each new situation that are easily adaptable

 © Substitute Teacher Training Institute

to different environments.

One of the most repeated admonitions to substitute teachers from permanent teachers is *"Be positive and aggressive in taking control of the class, immediately!"*

Set the rules, first those of the teacher's, then the school's, and finally yours . . . always be sure you know the rules, so you can have the students adhere to them.

Interestingly enough, most classroom teachers do not care if their class likes you. Their main concern is that you do whatever is necessary to have an orderly and productive time while you are there. If the students are disorderly in the halls, classroom or at an assembly, the teacher feels it reflects poorly not only on you, the substitute, but on them as well.

Things that a Substitute Teacher Can Do for the Permanent Classroom Teacher

1. Follow the lesson plans, do not have a free day.

2. Leave detailed notes for each class throughout the day, explaining how much work was accomplished, discipline problems, helpful students, etc.

3. Maintain control of the class.

4. Correct the work completed by the students during the day.

5. Keep students from getting into the teacher's desk.

6. Be consistent with existing class procedures.

7. Keep accurate absence reports.

8. Leave student work organized by class hour for the permanent teacher.

9. Follow lesson plans as carefully and closely as possible.

10. Make sure supplies are not lost or stolen.

11. Enforce discipline policies.

12. Be prepared with fill-in activities

13. Leave the classroom clean and orderly.

Follow the Lesson Plans

Over 75% of the teachers surveyed, reported that they spend 45 minutes or more writing lesson plans in preparation for a substitute teacher. Is it any wonder that teachers expect their outlined plan to be followed? Not knowing who the substitute will be and not knowing their level of experience, explains why most teachers feel so strongly about having things ready for their class.

Most teachers take the time to leave detailed plans that should be followed. One clever substitute teacher lists the agenda prepared by the permanent teacher on the board and tells the class, *"If there is time after we get the required work done, I have brought some fun activities for the class."* Not surprisingly, this particular substitute teacher is called upon often because permanent teachers know the work will get done and the students will have the opportunity to participate in some fun educational activities.

On the other hand, you may enter a classroom where you are unable to locate the lesson plans or necessary materials. Whatever the challenge may be for that particular day, your best approach is to act quickly, quietly, calmly, and with confidence. Be sure to have some items in your **Super Sub Pack** that can help you.

Pulling from your "Bag of Tricks" (when appropriate)

Having stated the importance of following the lesson plans, we encourage you to "do your own thing" when appropriate. As we interviewed permanent teachers, their first directive was to follow the lesson plan. When we suggested that substitute teachers could present their own fun and educational activities, they were ecstatic about having substitute teachers who were prepared with extra and alternative plans. You can become very proficient at presenting stimulating activities and discussions. Take advantage of this opportunity!

Professionalism

Substitute teachers are expected to maintain the same professional and ethical standards as permanent teachers. Professionalism is a vast expectation and one that is very important to the substitute teacher who wants to excel and enjoy their chosen profession. There are three key points to consider:

© Substitute Teacher Training Institute

a. Dress the Part

A professional looking substitute teacher arrives wearing clothes that are clean, pressed and appropriate for an educational setting. Various schools have differing dress codes, some require ties for men and dresses for women, others are more casual, and some schools even have a "dress down" day on Friday. Your best bet is to always dress in good taste, keeping with the dignity of the profession. You can always check with the district office or school, if there are any questions.

b. Be Positive

Permanent teachers care about the students in their classes. They know each student's individual strengths and weaknesses, and will want to see those areas handled appropriately. They hope the substitute teacher can appreciate the good in their students and bring out the best in them.

Permanent teachers urge substitute teachers to be aware of how small things, like using a normal voice, can affect the students in the class. Substitute teachers are also encouraged to use praise and have an upbeat attitude. When a substitute teacher uses good judgment, avoids criticism, and adapts to circumstances in a positive way, the teacher becomes a good role model for both the students in the class and other teachers.

A mature and well liked substitute teacher commented, *"I just try to relax, smile, and enjoy the day. I do my best and don't worry if things don't go exactly as planned."*

c. Respect the Students

Students resent a teacher who talks down to them and they may even act out. One substitute teacher noted, *"If I respect the students' rights by being fair and listening to their opinions, they will usually do the same for me."*

Treating the students as individuals is important. When needed and appropriate, talk "one-on-one" with students who are misbehaving. Do not blame the whole class, or punish the group for the misdeeds of a few. It is best to reprimand in private, and reward in public.

Leaving a Note for the Permanent Teacher

Teachers receive messages during the day over the intercom, on their computer, and on notes. Returning teachers appreciate it when you keep track of these messages and leave them on their desk.

Reporting the activities and events of each class is also an important end of the day activity. Write down what you think the teacher should know the next day, in terms of work completion, problems, significant incidences and successes. You may wish to use the form provided on page 200 of the appendix, for reporting such events to the permanent teacher.

In Conclusion

Teachers have high expectations of others who come into their classroom. Always remember that you are valued and an important part of the educational system. Never diminish your role as a substitute teacher. Teachers appreciate having a person come into their classroom who is caring and capable. By being prepared, poised, and professional, you will greatly reduce the stress on the teacher, students, and yourself.

Many school districts have prepared checklists for their substitute teachers to follow each day. We have taken the best from the best, listing them below and in the appendix.

At Home:

❑ Dress neat, clean, and appropriately for the teaching assignment.

❑ Enter the school enthusiastic and serious about your role.

❑ If possible, arrive at the school at least 20 minutes prior to the beginning of classes.

❑ Be sure to take along your sense of humor, your **Super Sub Pack**, an objective for the day, two aspirin and a snack for yourself.

© Substitute Teacher Training Institute

Prior to entering the class:

- ❑ Report to the principal or the office to let them know you have arrived.

- ❑ Ask about the policies regarding students in the halls and student passes.

- ❑ Ask if there will be any special duties associated with the permanent teacher's assignment.

- ❑ Find out how to refer a student to the office.

- ❑ Look for the fire alarm and know the proper drill directions.

- ❑ Ask if there might be a student who has a medical problem.

- ❑ Obtain any keys that might be necessary.

- ❑ Find out how to report students who are tardy or absent.

- ❑ Find the locations of restrooms and the teacher's lounge.

- ❑ Ask the names of the teachers on both sides of your classroom and if possible, introduce yourself to them.

In the classroom:

- ❑ If possible greet your students as they come in the door.

- ❑ Enter the classroom with confidence, the first impression can take you a long way.

- ❑ If lesson plans are provided, follow them as closely as possible.

- ❑ If money needs to be collected, record the amount, the name of the student, and the purpose for the collection on a sheet of paper then turn it in to the office at the end of the school day.

❑ Locate the books, handouts, and papers that will be needed throughout the day.

❑ Study the seating chart or be prepared to make your own.

End of class:

❑ If a teacher has classroom sets that are used by the students, be sure to have them all returned before anyone in the class leaves. It is easier to locate one book or calculator in a class of 30, than trying to find it in the whole school at the end of 7 periods.

❑ Remind students of homework. It is often helpful to write it on the board.

❑ Have students clean their desks and the area around their desk.

End of day:

❑ Leave the desks, books, and classroom in good order.

❑ Turn in any money collected at the office.

❑ Fill out a "Substitute Teacher Report" and leave it with all other materials for the permanent teacher. A sample report form is located on page 200 of the appendix.

© Substitute Teacher Training Institute

Chapter 2

CLASSROOM MANAGEMENT
and ORGANIZATION

This chapter addresses, in detail, some key principles of successful classroom management, as well as provides you with specific tips to help in making tough teaching decisions. There isn't one "true" recipe that guarantees a good class all day long, but these guiding principles will help. With experience, you will devise strategies of your own for gaining students' cooperation and attention. Your awareness and self-evaluation will play a key role in having successful management and organizational skills.

The Foundation For Success
- Arrive early.
- Locate seating chart, lesson plans, and materials.
- Greet students at the door.
- Introduce yourself to the class.
- Identify class rules or establish your own.
- Stick to rules and lesson plans.

Getting Off To A Good Start

Whenever possible, arrive at your assigned school at least 20 minutes before classes begin. When you check in at the office, ask if there are any special instructions, "special needs" students or special events for the day. By arriving early, you will have ample time to review the teacher's plans for the day and possibly have a chance to meet the teacher next door, who could prove to become a good friend and ally as the day progresses.

Before class begins, review the teacher's plans and find the materials needed for the day. If the teacher's plans are not very clear or if you have questions regarding the plans or materials, ask the teacher next door. In case you arrive late (which can happen if you are called at the last minute), do the best you can to glance at the teacher's plans and get the lay-of-the-land before your first class arrives.

When the bell rings, it is a good idea to be standing at the door greeting the students or standing in the front of the room ready to receive the class. Even if you are late and need more time to figure out the teacher's plans, don't be fumbling through papers while the students are entering the class. Be prepared with paper, pencils, the class roll, and a student activity, such as a *Sponge Activity* found on page 51, to give you more time to sort out the lesson and materials.

Look ready for the day to start, because it has!

Observe the students as they enter the classroom. Most effective teachers will have a previously established routine with their students and you may see this routine begin as the students start each class period. They will probably find their seats and wait for you to give them directions. Occasionally you may encounter a classroom filled with excitement, energy, and possibly even chaos. Whatever the situation, it's time for you to get their attention and introduce yourself.

First . . . don't begin speaking until you have everyone's attention. Introduce yourself as their teacher for the day and explain the reason for the teacher's absence (if you so choose). Establish your credibility. Give them a brief resume of your experience: *"I am a teacher and I have taught in junior high and high school."*

Remember to state that you are a "teacher," not that you are a substitute.

Managing Behavior

It is important to establish your procedures at the beginning of class. It is not so important what the procedures are, but once you state them, stick with them. Firmness and consistency are the key.

Many teachers will have classroom rules posted, but in case you are unable to find any, be sure you are armed and ready with your own set of rules. A key factor in student adherence to rules, is to have them prominently displayed. You may want to list them on a large poster board or the chalkboard.

Classroom rules should be specific and operational, so the students can easily understand what they mean. Phrases such as "be cooperative," "respect others," and "be polite and helpful" are too general and take too much time to explain.

"Follow directions the first time they are given," is direct and covers a lot of territory. You can continually reinforce the students in a positive way each time they follow the directions by saying, *"Thank you for following my directions the first time they were given,"* or *"Thank you for raising your hand."*

Here are some tried and true suggestions for classroom rules:
- Follow directions the first time they are given.
- Raise your hand for permission to speak.
- Keep hands, feet, and objects to yourself.
- Always walk in the classroom and in the halls.
- No Put-downs.

Keep in mind that rules are not just for the sake of having rules. When making rules, compare them with these purposes for rules of conduct:

1) To maximize on-task behaviors and minimize off-task, especially disruptive behaviors.

2) To secure the safety and comfort of the learning environment.

3) To prevent the activities of the class from disturbing other classes and persons outside of the class.

4) To maintain acceptable standards of decorum among students, school personnel, and visitors to the school campus.

Once the rules and consequences have been established, adhere to them. Reinforce the behavior you want and do not condone behaviors that are inappropriate. When you see appropriate behavior, respond with specific praise using the student's name. You can also give out points, tickets, or any reward system you or the teacher have established. It is important to continually reinforce the behavior standards for the class.

Calling students by name helps get their attention and keeps them paying attention to your directions.

Effective permanent teachers have clear and concise procedures for how things are to be done. They have specific rules with consequences that students understand. They continually give genuine, positive reinforcement to students for following the rules. Be confident, firm, assertive, and positive in eliciting the behaviors you want from the students. With an established plan, you are better prepared to deal with difficult situations that may arise.

> *A person's name is to that person the sweetest and most important sound in any language.* — Dale Carnegie

Challenging Scenarios

Here are a few situations you might encounter with some suggestions on how to respond to them, in a calm, positive manner, thereby gaining student compliance. You may wish to discuss these or other scenarios with a group of fellow teachers or even write down your own ideas in the margins.

To plan ahead and have a course of action decided and ready to implement is the best way to prepare yourself for these types of situations.

Scenario 1: The Interrupter

When asking a question of the class, a student responds without raising their hand for permission to speak, or speaks out of turn when a student response is not called for.

Strategy: Reinforce the behavior you desire, ignoring the inappropriate behavior.

- **Step 1:** Do not respond to the disruptive student. Look positively at those who are raising hands, calling on one of them saying, *"Thank you for raising your hand,"* as they then proceed to answer the question.

- **Step 2:** When you ask the next question, continue to reinforce the students who are behaving appropriately and move closer to the student who is not cooperating. Do not acknowledge the student who is speaking out of turn. If you give in and let that student answer, you are actually reinforcing the inappropriate behavior.

© Substitute Teacher Training Institute

Generally after Steps 1 and 2, the non-compliant student will cooperate and raise their hand. It is important that you call on them as soon as they raise their hand, providing verbal reinforcement for the appropriate behavior.

Scenario 2: Refusal To Do Work

After being given an assignment students refuse to do their work. When you encourage them to complete the assignment they make a statement such as, *"You can't make me."*

Strategy: Agree and Disarm.

- Disarm the student by agreeing that they are correct and then restate your expectations and consequences if they are not met.

  Example: *"You are right, I can't make you complete this assignment, but I can expect you to have it completed before the end of class/tomorrow. I also expect you to remain quiet and not disrupt the other students who are choosing to complete the assignment at this time."*

* Note: Many times a refusal to do work is an indication that the student doesn't know how to complete the assignment. They would rather appear bad, than stupid. If you suspect this may be the case you may need to re-teach the concept before expecting them to complete the work.

Scenario 3: Not Following Instructions

You have instructed the class to open their math books to page 24. Two students are talking, laughing, and not following your directions.

Strategy: Reinforce the behavior you expect.

- Repeat the instructions focusing on the students who are following your directions, *"Thank you for following the directions, Andy,"* or *"I appreciate John, Mary and Joe for following my directions so quickly."* You can also give points or tickets to students who are following directions.

Strategy: Proximity

- It is a good idea to use proximity. In other words, "move toward the problem" while you are talking. Move closely to the non-compliant student(s), repeating the instructions for the whole class. Your change in proximity will generally elicit compliance.

Scenario 4: The Class That Won't Be Quiet

After being given a "no talking" assignment class members are talking to one another and won't be quiet.

Strategy: Re-evaluate the situation.

- Step back and take a look at why the students are talking. Perhaps they do not understand the assignment and are trying to figure it out together. Maybe something has happened at lunch that needs to be dealt with. If you find that this is the case you may need to deal with the disruptive event, re-teach the objective, or perhaps even restructure the assignment to be completed as a class or in groups.

Strategy: Restate the expected behavior, motivators, and consequences.

- You may not have been clear in communicating your behavior expectations for the assignment. It may be necessary to gain the attention of the entire class and restate these expectations.

Example: " *Many of you are not behaving appropriately during this assignment. Let me explain exactly what I expect. I expect feet on the floor, students facing forward, and absolutely no talking. If you have a question please raise your hand and I will come to your desk. Students who choose not to follow these instructions will be assigned the consequences outlined in the classroom rules (review the consequences).*"

Having restated your expectations, it is often helpful to then call on students and have them restate the expectations, motivators, and consequences.

© Substitute Teacher Training Institute

Scenario 5: Transitions

You find that it is taking more than one or two minutes to make the transition from one activity to the next.

Strategy: Make it a step-by-step process.

- Students often waste a lot of time going from one activity to another. Instructions that seem simple such as, *"Get ready for silent reading"* are in reality quite ambiguous. Students need to know five specific things to make a quick transition from one activity to the next.

1. What to do about the activity they are currently engaged in.

2. What to do with the materials they are using.

3. What new materials they will need.

4. What to do with these new materials.

5. How much time they will have to make the transition.

Example: *"Please finish your essay, make sure your name is at the top, and pass it to the front of the row. Then take out your silent reading book and begin reading. I expect everyone to be silently reading in two minutes."*

Scenario 6: Assemblies

The principal informs you when you arrive at the school that there will be an assembly that day.

Strategy: Have a plan.

- This seemingly pleasant break in the school day can turn into a nightmare for a substitute teacher who does not have a plan for managing the students during this activity. Here are some suggestions to help you survive the event with nerves still intact.

1. Find out the time, location, and whether or not the students will

need to bring chairs from the classroom. Also be sure to ask if there will be an altered class schedule due to the assembly.

2. Talk to permanent teachers. Many schools have specific procedures for going to and returning from an assembly, as well as assigned seating for each class.

3. If such procedures exist, familiarize yourself with them and do your best to follow them.

4. If there are no established procedures devise your own (i.e. walk in a single file line down the hall to the assembly, sit together as a class, return in a single file line, etc.).

5. Determine the specific behaviors you expect during the assembly, with consequences and rewards dependent on how these expectations are met. Beware of punishing the whole class for the misdeeds of a few; this can create a hostile environment with the students acting out against each other as well as you.

6. Teach or review with the students the procedures, expected behavior, and consequences or rewards associated with the activity.

Scenario 7: Re-focusing The Class

The class is not paying attention or resuming their studies after an assembly, fire drill, or other disruptive event.

Strategy: Get Right to Work

*   A delay in resuming class work will only make things worse. As soon as everyone is seated, give directions for getting back on task immediately.

Strategy: Incorporate and Redirect.

*   A common experience is a great foundation for a learning activity. Regardless of how unwelcome the disruption may have been, it is

© Substitute Teacher Training Institute

an experience the entire class is familiar with. Use the experience as the basis for the next lesson. For example, if it was a fire drill and you are about to study science, talk about which parts of the school would burn the fastest. If you are about to study math, have students calculate the approximate number of people in each room that would need to be evacuated and the number of transportation vehicles that would be needed for taking everyone home. If preparing a writing lesson, have the students write about what would happen if the school really did burn down.

Strategy: Captivate and Redirect.

- Sometimes the best way to deal with a disruption is to minimize the event by capturing and redirecting their attention. For example, after an exciting assembly, complete a fun activity that requires students to do something, such as a *General Interest Activity* from this book. Involving students in a fun learning activity will help them settle back down to the routine of the day.

Scenario 8: Getting A Group's Attention

The class is in the middle of or just finishing an activity, you need to get their attention to either give further instructions or close the activity.

Strategy: Lights Out.

- If you want the attention of the entire class in a hurry, simply walk to the light switch and flip the lights off then on again. Be prepared to begin speaking in the moment of surprised silence, when you have every one's undivided attention. If you wait too long to start talking, the class will begin discussing the lights going out and the event itself will become a real distraction.

Strategy: Whisper.

- Your first instinct in this scenario may be to raise your voice above the noise level of the room and demand attention. However, this can incur some unwelcome side effects. The students hearing you speak loudly will assume that it is O.K. for them raise their voices as well. A better strategy is to do the opposite of your instincts. Move to the front of the room and begin talking and giving instructions very quietly. As students hear you, they will be quiet and focus their attention on understanding what you are saying. The quieter the room becomes, the quieter your voice should become. Soon students who are still talking and interacting will instinctively begin to feel awkward about making noise in such a quiet atmosphere and will become silent also. When you have the attention of the entire class, you can then give the instructions they need to hear for what they are working on.

Example (to be spoken in a very quiet voice): *"If you can hear what I am saying please put your pencils down and turn around to face the front of the room. Place your hands on your desk and look to see if the person sitting next to you is listening and doing the same. Now please open your book to page 122. . . ."* Continue with these simple, silent activities until you have the attention of the entire class.

Scenario 9: Wrong Names / Wrong Seats

You are using a seating chart to call on students by name. You notice that several students are not responding to their name and you suspect they have switched seats.

Strategy: State The Facts.

• Make a statement to the effect that it is better for everyone involved if you know the student's correct names. This information would be vital in the case of an emergency and will also help to insure that the wrong student doesn't get in trouble when you write your report to the permanent teacher at the end of the day.

Scenario 10: The "You vs. Them" Class

You get the feeling that the whole class, or at least several of the students, have banded together to make the class as difficult as possible for you, the substitute teacher.

Strategy: Work Together.

• Most "You vs. Them" scenarios turn out to be a lose-lose situation

© Substitute Teacher Training Institute

for everyone involved. Take the initiative early in the class hour to do a teacher and student interactive activity. You might try an activity from the *General Interest* section of this book. Interact with the students, let them see that you have a sense of humor. Hopefully, once you break the ice, the rest of the class hour will go smoothly. Making the classroom a battleground for control will usually only make things worse.

Scenario 11: Inappropriate Language / Derogatory Remarks

A student uses profanity or makes a derogatory remark about you, another student, or the permanent teacher.

Strategy: You chose to break the rule.

- Hopefully the classroom rules and consequences, established at the beginning of the class, have provisions for dealing with this challenging situation — Implement them! You might say something like, *"Susan, you chose to break classroom rule number three. The consequence for doing so is that you will have your name on the board."* Do not ask the student why they said what they said (you really don't want to know), just acknowledge that the student chose to break a rule and state the consequence. Try not to take the remarks personally. Keep your cool. Concentrate on dealing professionally with the behavior and not letting your feelings cause you to behave inappropriately. Then dismiss the incident and resume class work as quickly as possible.

Strategy: Remove and Reprimand.

- In some situations it is best to remove the student from the classroom before dealing with the behavior. Calmly ask the student to please step out in the hall. Redirect the class to resume their work and go into the hall yourself. Stay calm and in control of the situation. State the rule that was broken or explain that their behavior was unacceptable in your classroom. State the consequences and go on to explain the consequences if the rule is broken a second time. Express your confidence in the student's ability to behave appropriately then both of you return to the classroom.

There are two words that can stop any protestations, from any student, and let you take control of the situation. These words are, "I understand." If a student says, "but that's not fair," you can say, "I understand, but that's the way it is." If a student says, "I hate you!" you can say, "I understand, however I am the teacher today and you are expected to follow my directions." Two simple words with which no one can argue.

Scenario 12: A Fight

You see two students yelling at each other, poised for a fist fight. Respond quickly and decisively. Do not hesitate to get help from another teacher or administrator.

Strategy: Quickly and Decisively.

- Verbal jousting can often be extinguished by a firm command from you as you move toward the problem saying, *"I need both of you to take a quiet seat,"* or *"Stop this right now and take a quiet seat against the wall."* Your voice and the authority it represents conveys your message.

Strategy: Firm But Not Demeaning.

- If students are engaged physically, you must quickly and with authority tell them to step back away from each other. Placing yourself between the students stops the engagement, but can be dangerous for you. Do not get angry, excited, or show a lot of emotion, this will compound the situation. By giving firm and positive directions, the students should respond and comply as requested.

ACT instead of REACT when confronted with inappropriate behavior.

 © Substitute Teacher Training Institute

Scenario 13: Threats

A student threatens you or another student. Threats are a very challenging scenario and the best strategy and response will vary with each situation. The most important thing you, as the teacher, must do is to stay calm and emotionally detached so you can realistically evaluate and professionally deal with the situation.

Strategy: Diffuse the situation, and then redirect the student's actions.

- A threat is often the result of an emotional response. Ignoring the student will probably invoke more threats, and perhaps even aggression. Responding with threats of your own may accelerate the confrontation. The sooner the threat is acknowledged and the situation diffused, the better. Once the student has calmed down you can then direct their actions to something constructive. If you feel the student needs to discuss the situation it is often wise to wait until after class, or refer them to a school counselor so that they can gain some emotional distance and perspective on the situation.

Example: *"I understand that you are very angry right now. However, I need you to sit down and begin completing page 112 in your language book. We can discuss this situation after class."*

Strategy: Get help!

- If you feel that you or any of the students are in danger of physical harm, stay calm and immediately send a student to elicit the help of a permanent teacher or administrator. After help has arrived and the situation is under control document the occurrence. Record what happened prior to the threat, what you said and did, what the student said and did, as well as the involvement or actions of anyone else in the situation.

Remember: The goal is to handle the situation, without the situation handling you.

Ten Variables That Affect Compliance

1. Descriptive Requests

   Requests that are positive and descriptive are better than ambiguous or global requests. *"Please sit in your chair facing forward and looking at me,"* is better than *"Please pay attention."*

2. Start Requests vs. Stop Requests

   Positive requests for a student to start an appropriate behavior are better than negative requests for a student to stop a misbehavior. *"Please start your math assignment,"* versus *"Please stop arguing with me."*

3. Question Format vs. Direct Requests

   The use of questions instead of direct requests reduces compliance. *"Would you please sit down?"* is less effective than *"You need to sit down."*

4. Two Requests

   It is better to give the same request only twice than to give it several times.

5. Distance

   It is better to make a request from up close (0-3 feet) than from longer distances (10 feet or from across the room).

6. Eye Contact

   Making eye contact helps to convey the message.

7. Volume of Request

   It is better to make a request in a soft, firm voice rather than a loud voice.

8. Time

   Give the student time to comply after giving a request (5 to 10 seconds). During this short interval, do not converse with the student, rather, look at the student, restate the request (if required) and wait for compliance.

9. Neutral vs. Emotional Requests

   It is better to respond to behavior in a calm and matter-of-fact way rather than to·respond in an emotional way such as, yelling, giving ultimatums, etc.

10. Reinforce Compliance

    It is easy to request a behavior from a student and then ignore the positive result. If you want more compliance, genuinely reinforce it.

© Substitute Teacher Training Institute

Emergency Procedures

In addition to managing the classroom, there are a few other procedures and precautions to consider as a substitute teacher:

- Since every building and classroom is different, it is important for you to know how to evacuate the class in the event of a fire drill or other emergency.

- Know where the nearest exit is, having a class list available to grab when you evacuate the building.

- If you hear the fire alarm or a message over the intercom, instruct the students to quickly and quietly leave the room in single file, heading for the exit door.

- Some classrooms now have an emergency "backpack" hanging by the door that can be grabbed upon exiting with the class.

- If you see an emergency "backpack," take it with you when you evacuate.

Note: The most important task is to evacuate all of the students and to have a class list of your students, since you will be the only one to account for them.

Accidents

Handle most classroom accidents with common sense. Students who are injured should be taken to the office where a secretary or school nurse can administer first aid. Don't fall into the "band-aid and ice trap," where students are continually asking to go to the office for ice or band-aids for fake injuries. Be sure you know how to handle a situation involving blood in the classroom.

Do not touch a student who is bleeding, even if you use gloves.

For example: If a student has a bloody nose or bleeding wound, hand them a tissue or paper towels. Instruct them to hold it on their wound, then take them to the office for further care. Call for a custodian to clean up blood in the classroom, they have the necessary materials to deal with the situation safely.

In Conclusion

Your goal as a substitute teacher is to provide continuity in education while the permanent teacher is absent.

Remember to require students to pay attention and to stay on task. You might require students to repeat your directions after you give them. Continually move about the room while students are completing seat work or during group activities, ensuring that all of the students are participating and completing their work.

Communicate to the students the importance of learning by providing them with feedback regarding their work. Feedback tells them how well they are doing, reinforcing the importance of each lesson. Allow time to review any independent work completed, checking to see if anyone is having difficulty. Collecting all student work, and correcting it if you have time, sends the message to the students that the work they are doing is very important.

At the end of each class, provide closure for the learning activities by reminding the students to complete necessary homework and hand in work that is due that day. Compliment the students on their academic achievements for the day, letting them know how much you enjoyed working with them. Allow time at the end of class for proper closure and cleanup.

Remember to report each class in a note to the teacher. Write down what you think the teacher should know the next day, in terms of work completion, problems, significant incidences, and successes. You may want to use the form on page 200 of this book. Teachers really appreciate hearing from you and are more likely to ask you back if they feel you are competent in handling difficult situations and using effective strategies to solve problems.

Your efforts to be early, organized, efficient, prepared, and to communicate expectations and procedures clearly, will result in a positive educational experience for both you and your students.

> Effective classroom managers don't always treat inappropriate behavior or difficult situations differently than ineffective managers, but they do deal with the problem sooner.

© Substitute Teacher Training Institute

Your Own Plan

List other classroom management and organizational techniques you have heard or read about. Use the form on page 26 to organize your own classroom management techniques.

1) _____

_____

2) _____

_____

3) _____

_____

4) _____

_____

5) _____

_____

6) _____

_____

7) _____

_____

8) _____

_____

9) _____

_____

10) _____

_____

11) _____

_____

Classroom Management Planning Sheet

Rules

1. _____

2. _____

3. _____

4. _____

5. _____

Consequences

Positive:

_____

_____

_____

Negative:

_____

_____

_____

Procedures

_____

_____

_____

_____

_____

_____

© Substitute Teacher Training Institute

Chapter 3

Advice and Ideas

Introduction

Have you ever been left with lesson plans that you had no idea how to carry out, or realized that you are spending a small fortune on good behavior rewards and thought to yourself, *"There must be a better way!"* There is! Chapter Three, *Advice and Ideas*, is filled with ideas and suggestions from the files of permanent and substitute teachers. It includes:

- suggestions for the contents of your *Super Sub Pack*

- ideas for presenting the permanent teacher's lesson plans

- brainstorming instructions

- 101 ways to praise student effort

and many other helpful hints from experienced teachers who have been there, done that, and have some great advice to offer.

Super Sub Pack

Your **Super Sub Pack** is like the spare tire you keep in the trunk of your car. You take it with you everywhere you go and hope you never need to use it. However, just in case things start to go "flat" you'll be glad it's there.

Suggested Super Sub Pack Contents

- The *Substitute Teacher Training Handbook*

- A package of colored markers or pencils

- Several ball point pens (red, blue, black)

- Pencils

- A roll of transparent tape

- A pair of scissors

- A needle and small spools of dark and light thread, plus a safety pin or two

- A mug and perhaps a tea bag or hot chocolate packet

- Your favorite "prop" (puppet, stuffed animal, etc.)

- A joke book, book of riddles, or book of Minute Mysteries

- A number cube for dice games

- A whistle

- Several Post-It note pads

- 5x8 cards

- Pencils, stickers, candy, or other rewards and motivators

- Gift wrapped mystery box

- Tickets for drawings and contests

- Headache Medicine

- Granola bar or other snack

© Substitute Teacher Training Institute

Lesson Presentation Ideas

WHEN SUBSTITUTING, YOU ARE EXPECTED TO COVER THE MATERIAL OUTLINED IN THE REGULAR TEACHER'S LESSON PLAN.

However, sometimes the lesson plan instructions are general and very nonspecific with regard to lesson presentation. Here are several techniques for presenting lesson plan instructions that can lead the way to covering the material in a positive and creative manner.

Lesson Plan: Have students read Chapter 18 and answer questions.

(1)   Pretest and posttest. Ask students to guess what will be covered before they start reading. Share ideas aloud and write down five facts or ideas as predictions. Afterward, conduct a posttest by checking the accuracy of their predictions.

(2)   Togetherness. Read the assignment orally with the students to find the answers. By making the assignment a class activity, you promote classroom cooperation.

(3)   Group effort. Divide the class into groups and ask each one to report on part of the reading later. This method is best used with material that does not require continuity to be meaningful.

(4)   Quiz Board. Give the assignment and tell the students that you will stop 15 minutes before the end of the period and establish a quiz board. Appoint three to five students or select volunteers to be members of the board. Ask them to come to the front of the room. The rest of the students pose questions to these students about the day's reading. After a certain number of questions have been answered, a new board may be selected. This technique works well for review. An added advantage is that you need not know the subject well in order to handle it.

Lesson Plan: Have the class write a composition about X Y Z.

How to begin? The best move is to make the start interesting, challenging, and fun.

(1)   To make any topic more meaningful, encourage students to relate to it personally. One way is to write sentence starters that use the students' natural speech patterns, such as, "I wish," "I like," or "I'm glad I'm allowed to."

(2)   If the students are assigned to write a story, suggest that they first decide on a cast of characters, a setting, a time, etc. as a class. By doing the groundwork together, the students will be "into" the story before they lift a pencil.

(3)   If the assignment is an essay, consider using the "buzz group" technique. Ask students to say whatever comes to mind about the topic and write their ideas on the board in some quick abbreviated form. When everyone has had a chance to study the list, students can begin to write using whatever "buzzing" ideas they wish.

(4)   Whatever the topic, propose that the students write free association word lists about it. Tell them to start with the given word, such as freedom, pets, or winter, and add up to ten other words that immediately come to mind about the key word. Then the students can write their own compositions.

(5)   Before students start to write, initiate a values clarification exercise that will help students relate an abstract subject to their own lives. For example, if the topic is "conservation of electricity," have the students start by listing five electrical gadgets or appliances they use that they could do without. Record their answers on the board. From this specific exercise the students can move on to the broader issue.

Lesson Plan: The class has a test tomorrow. Have them study and review.

This sounds easy, but often isn't. Although you may not know the material the class has been studying, you can conduct a review session in several ways.

---

(1) Try a game format for drill material, such as spelling, number facts, state capitols, or vocabulary. Use familiar games like tic-tac-toe, categories, etc.

(2) Have pairs or small groups of students make up model tests. Assign one group true and false questions, another multiple choice questions, etc. Spend the last part of the period going over the questions. Ask each group to read their test, while the rest of the class ponders the answers.

Lesson Plan: Discuss topics A B C with class.

This can be most challenging! The students have been dealing with the topic and you have not. The following methods show how you lead the discussion constructively:

(1) Have one student lead the discussion or call on two or three students.

(2) Have the class spill out all sorts of ideas related to the discussion topic. Do not judge the ideas — anything goes! Just encourage the students to speak their minds. After about five minutes, start the discussion again, this time arranging their ideas in a more orderly fashion.

(3) If the topic is controversial, divide the class into sections, each representing a special-interest group. During the discussion, each group will give its point of view on the subject.

Lesson Plan: Show the film or filmstrip, then discuss.

Once the lights are off, this kind of assignment can turn into a disaster, but you can develop it into a delight.

(1) To heighten student interest in the audiovisual materials, use the same technique as that of the pretest and posttest. Introduce the exercise with a comment such as, *"If you were making a movie about China, what would you include?"* As they watch, have

students check their lists against the film. How does the film compare to the students' expectations?

(2)   As students watch, have them write down three questions that are answered in the film or video then exchange questions with another student after the presentation.

Keep in mind that with audiovisual materials it is crucial to get the students to be active, not passive, viewers.

Once you start using some of these techniques you will learn what works, when and where. Your confidence will grow. Remember, substituting is challenging, fun, and a potential opportunity for very good teaching to take place!

Adapted from the Substitute Teacher Handbook of the Scottsdale Public School District No. 48.

Scottsdale, AZ .

© Substitute Teacher Training Institute

Brainstorming

"Brainstorming" is an essential part of teaching creativity and the problem-solving processes that form the basis for active learning.

There are four simple rules that help make the brainstorming process a peaceful and orderly one. Teach these **"DOVE"** rules to the students:

D **Don't judge others' ideas -- evaluation comes later.**
O **Original and offbeat ideas are encouraged.**
V **Volume of ideas -- as many as possible in the time limit.**
E **Everyone participates.**

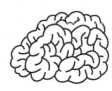

It is very common for students to run out of ideas in a short time. This is called "hitting the wall." Help students keep thinking, because the most interesting and unusual ideas often come after the immediate and obvious ones have been expressed. You may have a student read their list in order to help others start thinking about other ideas. Remind students that it is okay to "piggyback" on someone else's ideas. Often a really unique idea from one person can spark another good idea in someone else.

It is important in "brainstorming" to limit the time. A shorter time limit is better than one that is too long. One to three minutes is usually about right, occasionally up to five minutes might be needed. It is better to use a short time and extend the activity than to have the students lose interest.

"Brainstorming" warm-ups are very useful when teaching students about creativity. "Brainstorming" new and crazy uses for an object teaches students to be flexible in their thinking. The following examples work well:

- Brainstorm uses for a pencil.
- Brainstorm uses for a brick.
- Brainstorm all of the things that would be in the perfect classroom.

"Brainstorming" can be used to introduce a topic. "Brainstorming" at the beginning of a lesson is a good way to assess what students know about the topic, as well as being a good way to channel their thinking into the lesson.

Depending on the topic of the lesson, brainstorm attributes or facts that are related.

- Brainstorm things that are red (or read).
  - . . .   things in your home that are man-made, things that are natural.
  - . . .   things that are in the classroom that are geometric shapes.
  - . . .   things that live in the ocean, names of birds or flowers, insects, etc.

"Brainstorming" can also be used to help students evaluate an idea. For example, brainstorm all of the possible consequences:

- What if a light bulb that lasted 20 years was invented?
- What if the sun didn't shine for a year?
- What if students were all required to wear school uniforms?
- What if school busses were allowed to have advertising on them?
- What if you ran for school president and you won?
- What if your mother let you eat all of the junk food you wanted?

"Brainstorming" is used very effectively as one of the steps in problem-solving and solution-finding situations:

- What problems might you have if you came home from school and you were locked out of the house?
- What might happen if an earthquake destroyed your city?
- What are a variety of ways that you can prepare for a test?

"Brainstorming" is the first step. After many ideas have been generated, it is time to use those ideas to advance the objectives of the lesson. For example, if you brainstormed the consequences of eating all of the junk food you wanted, a lesson on nutrition might follow.

Evaluation of brainstormed ideas should not happen during the "brainstorming" process. If someone says, *"Boy, that won't work,"* then ideas are squelched and some students will stop participating. If evaluation is a step you want to use, it comes later after all ideas have been freely given.

© Substitute Teacher Training Institute

101 Ways To Say "GOOD JOB!"

Everyone knows a little praise goes a long way in the classroom. Whether it is spoken or written at the top of a student's paper, praise reinforces good behavior and encourages quality work. But the same traditional phrases used over and over can sound rehearsed and become ineffective. Here are 101 variations of ways to give praise, show interest, and offer encouragement:

1. You've got it made.
2. Super!
3. That's right!
4. That's good!
5. You are very good at that.
6. Good work!
7. Exactly right!
8. You've just about got it.
9. You are doing a good job!
10. That's it!
11. Now you've figured it out.
12. Great!
13. I knew you could do it.
14. Congratulations!
15. Not bad.
16. Keep working on it, you're improving.
17. Now you have it.
18. You are learning fast.
19. Good for you!
20. Couldn't have done it better myself.
21. Beautiful!
22. One more time and you'll have it.
23. That's the right way to do it.
24. You did it that time!
25. You're getting better and better.
26. You're on the right track now.
27. Nice going.
28. You haven't missed a thing.
29. Wow!
30. That's the way.
31. Keep up the good work.
32. Terrific!
33. Nothing can stop you now.
34. That's the way to do it.
35. Sensational!
36. You've got your brain in gear today.
37. That's better.
38. Excellent!
39. That was first class work.
40. That's the best ever.
41. You've just about mastered that.
42. Perfect!
43. That's better than ever.
44. Much better!
45. Wonderful!
46. You must have been practicing.
47. You did that very well.
48. Fine!
49. Nice going.
50. Outstanding!
51. Fantastic!
52. Tremendous!
53. Now that's what I call a fine job.
54. That's great.
55. You're really improving.
56. Superb!
57. Good remembering!
58. You've got that down pat.
59. You certainly did well today.
60. Keep it up!
61. Congratulations, you got it right!
62. You did a lot of work today.
63. That's it!
64. Marvelous!
65. I like that.
66. Cool!
67. Way to go.
68. Now you have the hang of it!
69. You're doing fine.
70. Good thinking.
71. You are learning a lot.
72. Good going.
73. I've never seen anyone do it better.
74. That's a real work of art.
75. Keep on trying!
76. Good for you!
77. Good job!
78. You remembered!
79. That's really nice.
80. Thanks!
81. What neat work.
82. That's "A" work.
83. That's clever.
84. Very interesting.
85. You make it look easy.
86. Good thinking.
87. Muy Bien! (very good in Spanish)
88. That's a good point.
89. Superior work.
90. Nice going.
91. I knew you could do it.
92. That looks like it is going to be a great paper.
93. That's coming along nicely.
94. That's an interesting way of looking at it.
95. Out of sight.
96. It looks like you've put a lot of work into this.
97. Right on!
98. Congratulations, you only missed . . .
99. Superb!
100. It's a classic.
101. I'm impressed!

Verbal Guidance

Throughout the day a teacher will need to convey instructions, warnings, directions, reprimands, and encouragement to students. Of the many ways to convey these messages, the most common is by speaking directly to the student or students. To be most effective verbal guidance should be brief, firm, and positive.

SAY:	DO NOT SAY:
Talk in a quiet voice.	Don't shout.
Use both hands when you climb.	You will fall if you don't watch out.
Climb down the ladder.	Don't jump.
Keep the puzzle on the table.	Don't dump the puzzle pieces on the floor.
Turn the pages carefully.	Don't tear the book.
Be sure the ladder is safe.	Be careful, you might fall.
Sit on your chair.	Don't rock in your chair.
Time to go inside.	Are you ready to go inside?

You will find it necessary to acquire techniques in keeping with your personality. However, the following general rules should be observed.

DO

1. Speak in a calm, kind voice.

2. Speak directly to the student, do not call across the room.

3. Speak in short, meaningful sentences which the student can understand.

4. Try to express your request in a positive way.

5. Keep your voice and facial expressions pleasant.

DO NOT

1. Make fun of the student.

2. Give students a choice if they cannot have one.

3. Compare the student with another, *"Look at how many questions Susan has completed."*

Adapted from: "Guidance of the Young Child," by Louise M. Langford.

© Substitute Teacher Training Institute

Low Cost / No Cost Rewards and Motivators

In the ideal classroom all of the students would be internally motivated to behave appropriately and work hard on every assignment. However, this is not usually the case. Many substitute teachers experience success in motivating classes by providing rewards. Below are several ideas for low or no cost rewards and motivators, as well as guidelines on how to use them effectively.

- Certificates: Photocopy blank certificates (such as those found on pages 39 and 40) to be filled out and given as prizes for classroom activities.

- Pencils and Paper Clips: Colorful variations of these school supply basics are well received at any grade level for contest winners. They can often be purchased very inexpensively at discount and dollar stores.

- Candy: Always a favorite, but be cautious when using it. Some students may have diabetes or other health conditions which do not allow them to enjoy this reward. In addition many state health codes require that candy be individually wrapped. If you do give out candy in the classroom be sure that the wrappers are disposed of properly.

- End of Class Activity: The promise of a fun activity later in the day will often motivate students. Remember that being "fun" is usually anything that is different from the routine of an ordinary day.

- Guessing Jar: Fill a jar with pennies, marbles, beans or M&M's. Next to the jar place a box for students to place their guesses as to how many of the item are in the jar. Recognize students who are on task, setting a good example, or working hard, by giving them a slip of paper to write their name and guess on. The more times they are recognized for good behavior throughout the class, the more chances they will have to "guess." At the end of the class reveal the total number of items in the jar and award a prize to the student whose guess was the closest.

- Talk Time: Often students enjoy moving to another seat and being allowed to sit and talk with friends during the last five minutes of class. To insure an orderly classroom, you may need to insist that the students select their new seat and then not be allowed to get up until the class is over.

Establish rewards and motivators not as "bribes to be good" but as goals that students can work toward and achieve through good behavior and diligent effort.

© Substitute Teacher Training Institute

Certificate of Award

_____
Name

did an outstanding job _____
today in class!

_____   _____
Date   Teacher

Certificate of Award

_____
Name

did an outstanding job _____
today in class!

_____   _____
Date   Teacher

Certificate of Award

_____
Name

did an outstanding job _____
today in class!

_____   _____
Date   Teacher

Congratulations . . .

_____
Name

Was a Winner in the _____ Contest Today!

_____   _____
Date   Teacher

Congratulations . . .

_____
Name

Was a Winner in the _____ Contest Today!

_____   _____
Date   Teacher

Congratulations . . .

_____
Name

Was a Winner in the _____ Contest Today!

_____   _____
Date   Teacher

Hints & Suggestions from Substitute Teachers

1. Know the teacher who is next door. Introduce yourself so you can call on someone for an answer for your questions about schedules or material for the class.

2. When students need to go to the media center to get or return a book, send only one student at a time. Then, when the first student returns a second may go.

3. If there is no seating chart left by the teacher, quickly make one. It is much easier to maintain discipline when you can call a student by name.

4. If a student doesn't respond when you call him/her by name, you may suspect the students have switched seats. Let them know it is better to have the correct names so the wrong student doesn't get in trouble and written about to the regular teacher.

5. Do not let a student start any name calling or being rude to other students. It is much easier to stop a disagreement at the verbal stage before it escalates to pushing or a fight.

6. Try to get in the hall between classes. It is a good idea to stand in the doorway so you can keep one eye on the hallway traffic and the other on the students coming into the classroom. If the students see a teacher they are less likely to start a fight or cause trouble.

7. Have a couple of extra pens or pencils with you for students who have forgotten and would rather go to their lockers and walk the halls than be in class.

8. If you do give a student a pen or pencil and you would like it back, be sure to ask for his/her lunch card, drivers license, or something that they will be sure to remember they want back. Many students forget to return things at the end of class.

9. Only one student to the rest room at a time. The next can go when the first comes back. This way you are not the bad guy.

10. Try to have the name of one or two trustworthy students who will tell you the truth and help out in the class.

11. Never let a class go early for lunch or the next class unless the teacher or the next door teacher says it is okay. Some schools have very strict rules about this.

12. Never let a student have a pen without an ink cartridge. It will possibly be used as a spit ball thrower.

13. Do not let the students use the phone in the classroom. Have them use the phone in the office.

14. Do not discuss the teacher's class with other people, especially out of school. You are a professional and shouldn't discuss individual students or problems. If you need to talk to someone about a problem talk to the principal.

15. Keep your opinions about students to yourself.

16. Be neat in your appearance.

17. Follow the lesson plans the teacher has left, supplement with your own materials when necessary.

18. Correct the students' class work for the day if possible.

19. Even though a few students can upset your plans, try to find out the names of the students who have been good or helpful and let the teacher know about them also.

20. Most students will know what needs to be done, but there will be some who will question your plans or authority. It is better not to argue. Instead say, *"I know this may not be the way Mr. Smith does it, but this is the plan for today."*

 © Substitute Teacher Training Institute

21. If you are not sure how the teacher wants an assignment done, ask another teacher or devise your own plan. Then be sure to leave a note for the regular teacher telling what you assigned.

22. Be assertive so the students don't feel they can manipulate your decisions and authority. You can use statements such as:
    I need you to start reading now.
    I want everyone to pass their papers forward.
    I don't need...
    I don't want...

23. Don't let the students manipulate you by protesting or saying, we never do that. Remain in control with statements such as, *"I know it can be hard to have a sub, but for today we will read aloud instead of silently."*

24. Walk around the room. Don't just sit by the desk, especially during homework, class work, or during a test. The students will be less likely to talk or cheat when you are close by.

25. Don't let them wear hats during a test. Some students have been known to write answers in the brim.

26. Don't try to catch a student by pulling his arm or his clothes. He could fall and you could twist his arm, or rip his clothes.

27. Don't let any student have a knife. Have them give it to you or have them go to the office. If a student has a nail file and jabs it at another student, consider that a weapon and have him give it to you.

28. Do not touch the blood of a bleeding child. Use a napkin, towel, or a cloth to cover the cut. Have the student put his hand on the cut, until you can get to water or the nurse.

29. If a teacher has classroom calculators which are used by the students, be sure to have them all returned before the entire class can leave. It is easier to locate one book or calculator in a class of

30 than trying to find one in the whole school. Hopefully the calculators or books are numbered and they have been assigned to be given out in order so you know who has the missing book.

30. Don't make statements lightly — students remember!

31. Maintain a sense of humor. Sometimes smiling or laughing with (not at) students can diffuse a potentially explosive situation.

32. Be consistent. This eliminates students "begging" for special favors.

33. Don't "back a student into a corner" — always provide a way out of a power struggle.

34. Don't take negative comments personally.

35. Avoid power struggles by negotiating so BOTH get what they want.

36. Don't criticize or embarrass students in front of others.

37. Find a way to reward yourself at the end of every day.

38. Say what you mean and mean what you say.

39. Know when to ask for help.

40. The best laid plans may not succeed — always have alternatives.

© Substitute Teacher Training Institute

Advice from Students

- Trust us.

- Be fair to everyone.

- Punish only the troublemakers.

- Make learning fun.

- Give us our assignment and let us go to work.

- Allow study time in class.

- Show concern and be willing to help with assignments.

- If I raise my hand, don't ignore me.

- You can be both strict and nice.

- Don't yell.

- Be straightforward with us.

- Be organized.

- Speak quietly and be patient.

- Give us something to work towards.

- Leave your personal life at home.

- Think positively of every student.

- Speak clearly.

- Be reasonable in your expectations.

- Have a sense of humor.

- Follow through with promises and consequences.

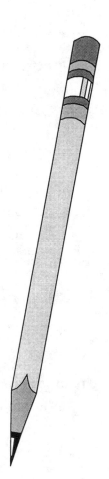

Getting A Permanent Job!

Many substitute teachers are working towards the goal of getting a permanent teaching assignment and classroom of their own. If you are such a substitute, on the next two pages are some suggestions that might help.

- **Be Proactive**

Meet with principals and district personnel early in the year to let them know that you are excited about working in the district and hope to at some point be offered a permanent teaching position. Let your intentions be known.

- **Be Available**

Districts are looking for dependable people. Once you have signed up to substitute, try to be available to teach whenever you are needed. Your willingness to fill in at the "last minute" will make a lasting favorable impression on those who will be making personnel decisions later in the year.

- **Be Professional**

You are a teacher in the school district, you should act, dress, and speak accordingly. Arrive early and stay late. Volunteer to help with after school activities. If your intentions to become a permanent teacher are known, you will be evaluated for this position in everything you do and say throughout the school year.

- **Don't Criticize**

Anything negative you say about a school, principal, or teacher will eventually come back to haunt you. Stay positive and sincerely compliment those around you whenever possible. If you can't say anything nice, don't say anything at all.

 © Substitute Teacher Training Institute

- **Be Confident**

Walk tall, act proud, but don't be overbearing.

- **Ask For Evaluations**

When appropriate, ask for evaluation forms or letters of support to be filed at the district office. Many times only negative evaluations are filled out and sent in.

- **Learn From Experience**

Don't assume that one bad experience or evaluation will take you out of the running. Learn from the experience, ask for advice from other teachers or principals.

- **Grow Professionally**

Attend workshops sponsored by the district. Some districts even invite substitute teachers to attend inservices scheduled for permanent teachers. You may also consider subscribing to current education journals or magazines, this illustrates that you are serious about a career in education and want to stay current with what's happening in the profession.

- **Get To Know The District**

One of most commonly used phrases in prospective teacher interviews is, *"Are you familiar with . . ."* By illustrating your knowledge of special programs, textbooks used, or the mission statement of a district you show that you are interested and up to date on what's going on within the district Applicants who are familiar with the mechanics of the district have a better chance of getting a job because the district recognizes that they are ready to go to work and begin contributing to the district's success without requiring extensive training and orientation.

Chapter 4

Activities and Lessons

There will be situations when the permanent teacher for some reason cannot leave lesson plans, when the plans that are left are impossible to decipher, or too short for the time available. These situations leave you with the dilemma of having to fill class time with manageable and worthwhile activities. Every good substitute teacher will have some tried and true activities which work without fail. Some such activities can be found in this book and kept in your *Super Sub Pack.* They will keep the students occupied in a positive manner, and learning at the same time.

The activities and lessons in this section have been arranged according to the following subjects:

- **General Interest**
- **Art**
- **English Literature**
- **Foreign Language**
- **Geography**
- **Government**
- **History**

- **Language Arts**
- **Math**
- **Music**
- **Science**
- **Speech / Drama**
- **What's Your Future?**

© Substitute Teacher Training Institute

In each section are filler activities, teacher directed lessons, and student worksheets. Time required and materials needed will vary. For reference purposes a table of contents listing each activity in the book is located in the appendix on page 197. By familiarizing yourself with a variety of ideas from various disciplines and assembling the necessary materials, you will be prepared for whatever teaching assignment you may encounter.

Suggestions for Implementing Activities and Lessons

- Contents are arranged by topic, however many lessons are appropriate for several different subjects. By familiarizing yourself with all of the lessons, you will be able to make the best use of all that this book has to offer.

- The worksheets and activities in this chapter are designed to stimulate thinking, and provide practice in deduction, as well as to enhance the standard core curriculum. Try to convey them as an opportunity to learn something new, rather than as an evaluation of what students should already know.

- Consider letting students work in groups to complete assignments, or work independently then in groups for the last five minutes. This removes some of the extreme pressure students feel to get the "right" answer.

- When using worksheets, prime the students with a discussion or brainstorming activity before handing them out. If their minds are in gear and they are already thinking about the topic, they will learn more as they process the information on the page.

- If you don't have the time or resources to photocopy student worksheets, consider completing them orally. Read the questions aloud and then allow students to respond. The material can be adapted to fit any time frame using this presentation style.

- Be specific in your instructions. If the assignment should be done without talking, say, "No Talking!" if it needs to be completed in 15 minutes let the students know.

- Allow enough time to check answers or share results at the end of an activity or assignment. If this is not possible, at least leave an answer key with the permanent teacher for students to check their work the next day.

- Answers for students to check their own work can be provided in a number of ways. The teacher can read them aloud at the end of the activity. An answer key can be taped to a desk or wall for students to consult, or answer keys can be photocopied and distributed when students finish the assignment.

- Always evaluate student work before returning it to them. Even just a couple of words at the top of the page, recognizes student effort, and validates the worth of the assignment.

- If you gave the assignment, it's your responsibility to correct and evaluate the students' work.

- Summarizing the activity helps to ensure that learning has taken place. One simple way to do this is to have students, or groups, take turns stating one new thing they learned from the activity.

© Substitute Teacher Training Institute

Secondary Sponges

A sponge activity is one that "soaks up" extra time. Students can complete the following activities independently, in groups, or as a whole class. In addition to the prompts below, sponges can also be developed to introduce, enhance, or compliment the lesson for the day.

1. How many different languages can you name?
2. List as many kinds of flowers as you can.
3. Name as many breeds of dogs as you know.
4. Write down a manufactured product for each letter of the alphabet.
5. You have five children. Make up their names.
6. Name as many restaurants as you can.
7. Scramble five vocabulary words from today's lesson, trade with someone, and unscramble them.
8. Write down as many cartoon characters as you can.
9. List as many different models of cars as you can.
10. How many baseball teams can you name?
11. Make a list of the 10 largest animals you can think of.
12. List as many breakfast cereals as you can.
13. Write down all of the different places you find sand.
14. List as many U.S. presidents as you can.
15. List as many states and their capitols as you can.
16. Name as many holidays as you can think of.
17. Write down all of the different flavors of ice-cream you can.
18. Name as many countries of the world as you can.
19. List all of the forms of transportation you can think of.
20. Name as many teachers at the school as you can.
21. Name the different sections of a newspaper.
22. Name all of the states that have the letter "E" in them.
23. List everything that is in your locker right now.
24. Name all of the different types of musical instruments you can.
25. If someone gave you $1,000 what are five things you would buy?

Old-Fashioned Riddles

A riddle usually hinges on one word or fact. Try these with your classes:

1. What is bought by the yard yet worn by the foot?   A carpet

2. What is full of holes, yet holds water?   A sponge

3. What is the longest word in the English language? Smiles. There is a mile between the first and last letter.

4. If eight sparrows are on a roof and you shoot at one, how many remain?

    None. They all fly away.

5. Why can't it rain for two days continually? Because there is always a night in between.

6. What speaks every language?   An echo

7. Why is Ireland the wealthiest country? Because its capital is always Dublin.

8. Why is a nose in the middle of a face? Because it is the scenter.

9. If a telephone and a piece of paper had a race, who would always win?

    The telephone, since the paper will always remain stationary.

10. Why should fish be well-educated? They are found in schools.

11. What is the difference between a jeweler and a jailer?
    One sells watches, and the other watches cells.

12. Which takes the least time to get ready for a trip: An elephant or a rooster?
    The rooster . . . He only takes his comb, but the elephant has to take a whole trunk.

13. Do they have a Fourth of July in England?

    Yes. (But it is not a holiday.)

          © Substitute Teacher Training Institute

14. Can a man living in Chicago be buried west of the Mississippi?

No. (He is living.)

15. How far can a dog run into the woods?

Halfway. (The other half he is running out.)

16. A farmer had seventeen sheep. All but nine died. How many did he have left?

Nine

17. A man has two coins in his hand. The two coins total fifty-five cents. One is not a nickel. What are the two coins?

A nickel plus a half dollar. (The other is a nickel.)

18. Take two apples from three apples. What have you got?

Two apples.

19. Four men can build four boats in four days. How long will it take one man to build one boat?

Four days. (Four men building four boats is the same as one man working sixteen days.)

20. Can you measure out exactly two gallons of water using only two unmarked containers? One of the containers will hold eight gallons and the other will hold five gallons.

Pour five gallons into the eight gallon can. Then repeat this until the eight gallon can is full. (Two gallons will be remaining in the five gallon can.)

Are They for Real?

Some literary characterizations have been so vivid that they have almost taken a place in history. On the other hand, some real people have lived such legendary lives that they seem almost fictional. Can you identify the following men and explain if they were fact or fiction?

1. Alexander the Great   7. Sherlock Holmes

2. King Arthur   8. Paul Revere

3. Paul Bunyan   9. Mark Twain

4. Lloyd George   10. Mike Fink

5. Johnny Appleseed   11. Marco Polo

6. Robin Hood   12. Ivan the Terrible

Who Invented That?

The names of some men who invented many of the things you use every day are familiar to you, but some of them may not be at all. Can you identify the inventor of the following items.

1. The sewing machine   Elias Howe

2. The phonograph   Isaac M. Singer

3. The television   Thomas Edison

4. The material called plastic   Emile Berliner

5. The sandwich   John Wesley Hyatt

6. The pin   Alexander Parks

                                            John Montagu

                                            Lemuel W. Wright

                    © Substitute Teacher Training Institute

Are They for Real? ANSWER KEY

1. Alexander the Great was fact. He was the King of Macedonia, lived 356-323 B.C., and was considered a military genius for his conquests of Greece, Egypt, and the Middle East.

2. King Arthur was fiction, the legendary King of Britain who presided over the Roundtable.

3. Paul Bunyan was fiction, a tall-tale hero of early-American fiction.

4. Lloyd George was fact. He was the Prime Minister of Great Britain during WWI.

5. Johnny Appleseed was fact. His real name was John Chapman. One of the original ecologists, he walked over the American countryside planting apple seeds.

6. Robin Hood was fiction. Though some authorities say the legendary charitable bandit of Sherwood Forest was based on a historical person, little evidence has been found.

7. Sherlock Holmes was the fictional detective to whom the solutions to tangled problems were "Elementary, my dear Watson." He was created by Sir Arthur Conan Doyle.

8. Paul Revere was fact, a silversmith and patriot of the American Revolution.

9. Mark Twain was fact, though his real name was Samuel Clemens. He was an American humorist and the author of Tom Sawyer and The Adventures of Huckleberrry Finn.

10. Mike Fink, though based on a real person, had so many tall-tales built around his career as a keel boat man that he must be considered fiction.

11. Marco Polo was fact. He was a Venetian who traveled through most of Asia on his trips in the thirteenth and fourteenth centuries.

12. Ivan the Terrible was fact. He was a Russian Czar who became noted for brutality and tyranny.

Who Invented That? ANSWER KEY

1. Elias Howe received credit for this invention after a lengthy patent dispute with Isaac M. Singer.

2. Thomas Edison is credited with the invention of the phonograph, but Emile Berliner developed the flat disc record, the lateral-cut groove, and a method of duplicating records.

3. There is no single inventor in the field of television. It is the result of many discoveries in electricity, electromagnetism, and electrochemistry.

4. Celluloid was the first of the synthetic plastics and was invented by John Wesley Hyatt following experiments done by Alexander Parkes. Hyatt was seeking material with which to make a better billiard ball.

5. The sandwich was invented by John Montagu, the Earl of Sandwich, because he was too busy gambling to take time out to eat a regular meal.

6. The ordinary pin with a solid head was first made on a machine invented by Lemuel W. Wright in 1824 in New Hampshire. Until then, the head of a pin was made by twisting fine wire into a ball and soldering it to one end of a sharpened wire.

© Substitute Teacher Training Institute

NAME _____

Word Puzzles I

Directions:

These puzzles represent expressions we use. Solve them by carefully noticing the positions of the words and pictures. Are they under, over, mixed-up, inside, or a certain size?

E K A KISSM	search and	NEFRIENDED	wear ――― long
egsg gesg segg sgeg	S M O K E	GIVE GET GIVE GET GIVE GET GIVE GET	cover ――― agent
NOT GUILTY STANDER	man ――― board	EZ ――― iiii	LM AL EA AE EM ML
BELT ――― HITTING	A D S L A	he { art	**T.V.**
ar up ms	**CHAIR**	TIRE	T O W N

―――

Utah State University   **57**

Word Puzzles II

Directions:

These puzzles represent expressions we use. Solve them by carefully noticing the positions of the words and pictures. Are they under, over, mixed-up, inside, or a certain size?

S O C K (inside I)	1,000, **1** 000	C O S T S (diagonal)	ground / feet feet / feet feet / feet feet
g o i g n / a r o d n u n (circles)	time time	stand / I	T O U C H (vertical)
FRIENDS standing/miss FRIENDS	WALKING	SOUP	ter very esting
r|e|a|d|i|n|g	b sick ed	LO head/heels VE	knee/lights
g r u / the block / n i n n	every|right|thing	R R / O O / A / D D / S S	i/8

© Substitute Teacher Training Institute

Word Puzzles I: ANSWER KEY

1. kiss and make up
2. search high and low
3. friend in need
4. long underwear
5. scrambled eggs
6. up in smoke
7. forgive and forget
8. undercover agent
9. innocent bystander
10. man overboard
11. easy on the eyes
12. three square meals
13. hitting below the belt
14. tossed salad
15. broken heart
16. black and white TV
17. up in arms
18. high chair
19. flat tire
20. downtown

Word Puzzles II: ANSWER KEY

1. sock in the eye
2. one in a million
3. rising costs
4. six feet underground
5. going around in circles
6. time after time
7. I understand
8. touchdown
9. mis-understanding between friends
10. walking tall
11. split pea soup
12. very interesting
13. reading between the lines
14. sick in bed
15. head over heals in love
16. neon lights
17. running around the block
18. right in the middle of everything
19. cross roads
20. I over ate

Under Construction

Time: 30 min. +

Objective: Students will develop a sketch for a teacher assigned construction project.

Materials: sketch paper, pencils,

Optional Materials: colored pencils, rulers, compasses, templates etc.

Advance Preparation: Determine the specific details of the project to be assigned.

In this activity students will be asked to complete a sketch for a construction project. The details, specifications, areas of emphasis, difficulty level, and nature of the project will be determined by the teacher.

Possible construction projects include the following:

- a kitchen
- a house
- a school
- a shopping mall

- a hotel
- a flower garden
- a new city park
- a new 100 home community

Potential areas of emphasis could include the following:

- drawing to scale
- color schemes
- cost efficiency

- creativity
- practicality

PROCEDURE:

1. Make sure all students are equipped with paper and pencils.

2. Explain the nature of the assignment, details of the constructions project and set a time limit.

© Substitute Teacher Training Institute

Example: *Today's assignment is to complete a sketch for a new resort hotel to be built in Las Vegas. The International Boating Association wants to develop a boat-theme resort featuring a 300 room hotel, swimming pool, tropical aquarium, large sand box, and outdoor restaurant. The resort wants to become "the" place for families to stay in Vegas. Your preliminary sketches need to be turned in by the end of the class hour and will be evaluated on the creativity of incorporating the "boat-theme" into the design.*

Distributing copies of the instructions or outlining key information on the board will eliminate the need for repeating the details of the assignment over and over again.

3. Monitor student work.

4. Collect and evaluate the finished projects.

You may want to photocopy or request permission to keep samples of excellent work to use as examples in other classes.

Business by Design

You have been selected to design the new business cards for *Tropical Island*, a company which grows and sells tropical plants.

The following information must be included on the card:

- Company Name
- Company Logo (which you design)
- Employee Name
- Employee Title
- Mailing Address
- Fax Number
- Telephone Number
- E-mail Address

The actual card size is:

2" by 3 1/2" but you can complete your design in the larger box below.

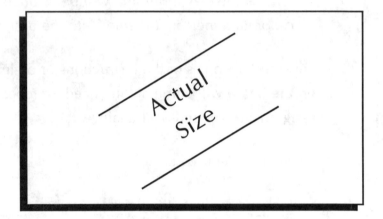

Your Design:

© Substitute Teacher Training Institute

Illustrators Wanted

An important part of many books are the illustrations. Colorful and creative images captivate audiences both young and old. Illustrate one of the poems below using colors and images which will capture the attention of readers and hold the attention of young listeners.

In Time of Silver Rain *by Langston Hughes*

In time of silver rain

The butterflies lift silken wings

To catch a rainbow cry,

And trees put forth

New leaves to sing

In joy beneath the sky

As down the roadway passing boys

And girls go singing, too,

In time of silver rain

When spring

And life are new.

Choosing Shoes *by Frida Wolfe*

New shoes, new shoes,

　Red and pink and blue shoes.

Tell me what would you choose,

　If they'd let us buy?

Buckle shoes, bow shoes,

　Pretty pointy-toe shoes,

Strappy, cappy low shoes;

　Let's have some to try.

Bright shoes, white shoes,

　Dandy-dance-by-night shoes,

Perhaps a little tight shoes,

　Like some? So would I.

　But

Flat shoes, fat shoes,

　Stump-along-like-that shoes,

Wipe them on the mat shoes,

　That's the sort they'll buy.

NAME _____

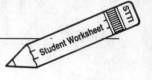

The Obscure Words of Art

Like any other discipline, Art has a vocabulary of its own. How savvy are you at deciphering its obscure terminology? Try to match the words below with the correct definition or description.

Tools of the Trade

_____ 1. stump

_____ 2. rigger

_____ 3. rib

_____ 4. adze

_____ 5. mahlstick

_____ 6. spline

_____ 7. graver

_____ 8. pantograph

A. a rod shaped engraving tool

B. a tool used in shaping ceramic pots

C. cigar-shaped tool used to blend or smudge charcoal, pencil, chalk, or crayon

D. a cutting tool used in sculpture to rough shape wood

E. a light wooden rod three or four feet long which painters use as a rest or support when executing detailed work

F. a device used to copy, enlarge, or reduce a work of art

G. narrow strip of flexible, transparent plastic used in mechanical drawings as a ruler for curved surfaces

H. a lettering brush half the width of a standard lettering brush of the same numbered size

Colors of Art

_____ 1. ceruse

_____ 2. cyan

_____ 3. magenta

_____ 4. bistre

_____ 5. chay

_____ 6. tumeric

_____ 7. weld

_____ 8. chartreuse

A. a brilliant yellow green

B. a yellow to reddish brown dyestuff

C. a brown pigment made by burning beech wood

D. deep blue

E. white lead

F. deep dark purplish blue, or bluish maroon

G. a natural red dyestuff obtained from the root of an East Indian plant

H. a bright yellow dye

© Substitute Teacher Training Institute

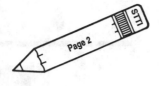

The Obscure Words of Art

Miscellaneous Art Terms

_____ 1. taboret

_____ 2. cachet

_____ 3. blot drawing

_____ 4. mastic

_____ 5. interlace

_____ 6. merz

__ 7. putto

_____ 8. thumbnail sketch

_____ 9. aquarelle

A. a rough sketch of very small proportions

B. small cabinet kept near an artist's drawing table or easel

C. an artistic invention made up of discarded materials (old bus tickets, candy wrappers, etc.)

D. an accidental blot or stain on a paper used to construct an imaginary landscape

E. a monogram or symbol used in place of a signature

F. the technique of painting in transparent water color

G. a chubby nude infant often depicted in art from the 15th century on

H. resin obtained from a tree used in the 19th century as a picture varnish

I. a pattern of art in which elements intercross and intertwine with one another

Tools of the Trade ANSWER KEY

1. stump   C. cigar-shaped tool used to blend or smudge charcoal, pencil, chalk, or crayon

2. rigger   H. a lettering brush half the width of a standard lettering brush of the same numbered size

3. rib   B. a tool used in shaping ceramic pots

4. adze   D. a cutting tool used in sculpture to rough shape wood

5. mahlstick   E. a light wooden rod three or four feet long which painters use as a rest or support when executing detailed work

6. spline   G. narrow strip of flexible, transparent plastic used in mechanical drawings as a ruler for curved surfaces

7. graver   A. a rod shaped engraving tool

8. pantograph   F. a device used to copy, enlarge, or reduce a work of art

Colors of Art ANSWER KEY

1. ceruse   E. white lead

2. cyan   D. deep blue

3. magenta   F. deep dark purplish blue, or bluish maroon

4. bistre   C. a brown pigment made by burning beech wood

5. chay   G. a natural red dyestuff obtained from the root of an East Indian plant

6. tumeric   B. a yellow to reddish brown dyestuff

7. weld   H. a bright yellow dye

8. chartreuse   A. a brilliant yellow green

© Substitute Teacher Training Institute

Miscellaneous Art Terms ANSWER KEY

1. taboret   B. small cabinet kept near an artist's drawing table or easel

2. cachet   E. a monogram or symbol used in place of a signature

3. blot drawing   D. an accidental blot or stain on a paper used to construct an imaginary landscape

4. mastic   H. resin obtained from a tree used in the 19th century as a picture varnish

5. interlace   I. a pattern of art in which elements intercross and intertwine with one another

6. merz   C. an artistic invention made up of discarded materials (old bus tickets, candy wrappers, etc.)

7. putto   G. a chubby nude infant often depicted in art from the 15th century on

8. thumbnail sketch   A. a rough sketch of very small proportions

9. aquarelle   F. the technique of painting in transparent water color

Masters of the Trade

You probably recognize the names of the artists listed below. But can you match the artist to one of their well known works and an event or characteristic of their life? In front of the artist column write both the Work of Art letter and Trivia number.

Artist	Work of Art	Trivia
_____ _____ Rembrandt	A. The Marriage of Giovanni	1. A persian known as the master of the miniature.
_____ _____ Monet	B. Sistine Madonna	2. Luncheon guests sometimes waited several hours while he painted the cook.
_____ _____ Leonardo	C. Anatomy Lesson of Dr. Tulp	3. He painted more than 100 self-portraits throughout his life.
_____ _____ Picasso	D. Book of Victory	4. He always signed his pictures in letters of the Greek alphabet.
_____ _____ Degas	E. Water-lily Series	5. The local barber came to the open field and cut his hair while he painted.
_____ _____ Renoir	F. The Three Dancers	6. Shot himself in a field and died two days later.
_____ _____ El Greco	G. Mona Lisa	7. He was forbidden to see his mother after the age of five.
_____ _____ Michelangelo	H. The Dancing Class	8. During World War I he designed scenery for Diaghilev's Ballets Russes.
_____ _____ David	I. The Burial of Count Orgaz	9. Before death he walked the streets of Paris alone, blind, and terrified of automobiles.
_____ _____ Rousseau	J. David	10. He played the violin for his friends and flute in the French Army Infantry Band.
_____ _____ Raphael	K. The Coronation	11. As a nobleman and aristocrat he could not accept money for his work.
_____ _____ Velazquez	L. Gabrielle With a Rose	12. He worked in Rome off and on for 70 years for seven different Popes.
_____ _____ Van Eych	M. Starry Night	13. Made distant and secret journeys to paint portraits of princesses for Philip the Good.
_____ _____ Bihzad	N. The Sleeping Gypsy	14. Drew 10 cartoons depicting scenes from the acts of the apostles; made tapestries.
_____ _____ Van Gogh	O. The Spinners	15. Twice his wife plead for and gained his freedom from prison.

© Substitute Teacher Training Institute

Masters of the Trade ANSWER KEY

		Artist	Work of Art	Trivia
C	3	Rembrandt	The Anatomy Lesson of Dr. Tulp	He painted more than 100 self-portraits throughout his life.
E	5	Monet	Water-lily Series	Made the local barber come to the open field and cut his hair while he painted.
G	7	Leonardo	Mona Lisa	He was forbidden to see his mother after the age of five.
F	8	Picasso	The Three Dancers	During World War I he designed scenery for Diaghilev's Ballets Russes.
H	9	Degas	The Dancing Class	Before death he walked the streets of Paris alone, blind, and terrified of automobiles.
L	2	Renoir	Gabrielle With a Rose	Luncheon guests sometimes waited several hours while he painted the cook.
I	4	El Greco	The Burial of Count Orgaz	He always signed his pictures in letters of the Greek alphabet.
J	12	Michelangelo	David	He worked in Rome off and on for 70 years for seven different Popes.
K	15	David	The Coronation	Twice his wife plead for and gained his freedom from prison.
N	10	Rousseau	The Sleeping Gypsy	He played the violin for his friends and flute in the French Army Infantry Band.
B	14	Raphael	Sistine Madonna	Drew cartoons depicting scenes from the acts of the apostles; made into tapestries.
O	11	Velazquez	The Spinners	As a nobleman and aristocrat he could not accept money for his work.
A	13	Van Eych	The Marriage of Giovanni	Made distant and secret journeys to paint portraits of princesses that Philip the Good.
D	1	Bihzad	Book of Victory	A persian known as the master of the miniature.
M	6	Van Gogh	Starry Night	Shot himself in a field and died two days later.

Great Minds Think Alike

Time: 30 minutes

Objective: Students will write the ending to a short story then compare their conclusion with that of the original author.

Materials: Copy of an original short story, paper, pencils

Advance Preparation: None

Procedure:

1.   Explain to students that you are going to read the beginning of a short story by Guy De Maupassant (or author of your choice) and then have them write the ending to the story. When everyone has finished writing, they will have the opportunity to share their writings and compare them to the conclusion written by the original author.

2.   Read the beginning of *The Necklace* (or other short story of your choice) aloud to the class (see page 71).

3.   Allow students 15 minutes to write a conclusion to the story.

4.   If time permits, invite students to share their conclusions with the class or in small groups.

5.   Read aloud the original ending to the story.

6.   Ask students to list similarities and differences between their conclusion and the author's conclusion at the bottom of their page and then turn it in for teacher evaluation.

                                                          © Substitute Teacher Training Institute

THE NECKLACE

GUY DE MAUPASSANT

She was one of those pretty, charming young ladies, born, as if through an error of destiny, into a family of clerks. She had no dowry, no hopes, no means of becoming known, appreciated, loved and married by a man either rich or distinguished; and she allowed herself to marry a petty clerk in the office of the Board of Education.

She was simple, not being able to adorn herself, but she was unhappy, as one out of her class; for women belong to no caste, no race, their grace, their beauty and their charm serving them in the place of birth and family. Their inborn finesse, their instinctive elegance, their suppleness of wit, are their only aristocracy, making some daughters of the people the equal of great ladies.

She suffered incessantly, feeling herself born for all delicacies and luxuries. She suffered from the poverty of her apartment, the shabby walls, the worn chairs and the faded stuffs. All these things, which another woman of her station would not have noticed, tortured and angered her. The sight of the little Breton, who made this humble home, awoke in her sad regrets and desperate dreams. She thought of quiet antechambers with their oriental hangings lighted by high bronze torches and of the two great footmen in short trousers who sleep in the large armchairs, made sleepy by the heavy air from the heating apparatus. She thought of large drawing rooms hung in old silks, of graceful pieces of furniture carrying bric-a-brac of inestimable value and of the little perfumed coquettish apartments made for five o'clock chats with the most intimate friends, men known and sought after, whose attention all women envied and desired.

When she seated herself for dinner before the round table, where the tablecloth had been used three days, opposite her husband who uncovered the tureen with a delighted air, saying; "Oh! the good potpie! I know nothing better than that," she would think of the elegant dinners of the shining silver, of the tapestries peopling the walls with ancient personages and rare birds in the midst of fairy forests; she thought of the exquisite food served on marvelous dishes, of the whispered gallantries, listened to with the smile of the Sphinx while eating the rose-colored flesh of the trout or a chicken's wing.

She had neither frocks nor jewels, nothing. And she loved only those things. She felt that she was made for them. She had such a desire to please, to be sought after, to be clever and courted.

She had a rich friend, a schoolmate at the convent, whom she did not like to visit; she suffered so much when she returned. And she wept for whole days from chagrin, from regret, from despair and disappointment.

One evening her husband returned, elated, bearing in his hand a large envelope.

"Here," he said, "here is something for you."

She quickly tore open the wrapper and drew out a printed card on which were inscribed these words:

The Minister of Public instruction and Madame George Ramponneau ask the honor of M. and Mme Loisel's company Monday evening, January 18, at the Minister's residence.

Instead of being delighted, as her husband had hoped, she threw the invitation spitefully upon the table, murmuring:

"What do you suppose I want with that?"

"But my dearie, I thought it would make you happy. You never go out, and this is an occasion, and a fine one! I had a great deal of trouble to get it. Everybody wishes one, and it is very select; not many are given to employees. You will see the whole official world there."

She looked at him with an irritated eye and declared impatiently:

"What do you suppose I have to wear to such a thing as that?"

He had not thought of that; he stammered:

"Why, the dress you wear when we go to the theater. It seems very pretty to me."

He was silent, stupefied, in dismay, at the sight of his wife weeping. Two great tears fell slowly from the corners of her eyes toward the corners of her mouth; he stammered:

"What is the matter? What is the matter?"

By a violent effort she had controlled her vexation and responded in a calm voice, wiping her moist cheeks:

"Nothing. Only I have no dress and consequently I cannot go to this affair. Give your card to some colleague whose wife is better fitted out than I.

He was grieved but answered;

"Let us see, Matilda. How much would a suitable costume cost, something that would serve for other occasions, something very simple?"

She reflected for some seconds, making estimates and thinking of a sum that she could ask for without bringing with it an immediate refusal and a frightened exclamation from the economical clerk.

Finally she said in a hesitating voice:

"I cannot tell exactly, but it seems to me that four hundred francs ought to cover it."

He turned a little pale, for he had saved just this sum to buy a gun that he might be able to join some hunting parties the next summer, on the plains at Nanterre, with some friends who went to shoot larks up there on Sunday. Nevertheless, he answered:

"Very well. I will give you four hundred francs. But try to have a pretty dress."

The day of the ball approached, and Mme Loisel seemed sad, disturbed, anxious. Nevertheless, her dress was nearly ready. Her husband said to her one evening:

"What is the matter with you? You have acted strangely for two or three days."

And she responded: "I am vexed not to have a jewel, not one stone, nothing to adorn myself with. I shall have such a poverty-laden look. I would prefer not to go to this party."

He replied: "You can wear some natural flowers. At this season they look very chic. For ten francs you can have two or three magnificent roses."

She was not convinced. "No," she replied, "there is nothing more humiliating than to have a shabby air in the midst of rich women."

Then her husband cried out: "How stupid we are! Go and find your friend Madame Forestier and ask her to lend you her jewels. You are well enough acquainted with her to do this."

She uttered a cry of joy. "It is true!" she said. "I had not thought of that."

The next day she took herself to her friend's house and related her story of distress. Mme Forestier went to her closet with the glass doors, took out a large jewel case, brought it, opened it and said; "Choose, my dear."

She saw at first some bracelets, then a collar of pearls, then a Venetian cross of gold and jewels and of admirable workmanship. She tried the jewels before the glass, hesitated, but could neither decide to take them nor leave them. Then she asked:

"Have you nothing more?"

"Why, yes. Look for yourself. I do not know what will please you."

Suddenly she discovered in a black satin box a superb necklace of diamonds, and her heart beat fast with an immoderate desire. Her hands trembled as she took them up. She placed them about her throat, against her dress, and remained in ecstasy before them. Then she asked in a hesitating voice full of anxiety:

"Could you lend me this? Only this?"

"Why, yes, certainly."

She fell upon the neck of her friend, embraced her with passion, then went away with her treasure.

The day of the ball arrived. Mme Loisel was a great success. She was the prettiest of all, elegant, gracious, smiling and full of joy. All the men noticed her, asked her name and wanted to be presented. All the members of the Cabinet wished to waltz with her. The minister of education paid her some attention.

She danced with enthusiasm, with passion, intoxicated with pleasure, thinking of nothing, in the triumph of her beauty, in the glory of her success, in a kind of cloud of happiness that came of all this homage and all this admiration, of all these awakened desires and this victory so complete and sweet to the heart of woman.

She went home toward four o'clock in the morning. Her husband had been half asleep in one of the little salons since midnight, with three

© Substitute Teacher Training Institute

other gentlemen whose wives were enjoying themselves very much.

He threw around her shoulders the wraps they had carried for the coming home, modest garments of everyday wear, whose poverty clashed with the elegance of the ball costume. She felt this and wished to hurry away in order not to be noticed by the other women who were wrapping themselves in rich furs.

Loisel detained her. "Wait," said he. "You will catch cold out there. I am going to call a cab."

But she would not listen and descended the steps rapidly. When they were in the street they found no carriage, and they began to seek for one, hailing the coachman whom they saw at a distance.

They walked along toward the Seine, hopeless and shivering. Finally they found on the dock one of those old nocturnal coupes that one sees in Paris after nightfall, as if they were ashamed of their misery by day.

It took them as far as their door in Martyr Street, and they went wearily up to their apartment. It was all over for her. And on his part he remembered that he would have to be at the office by ten o'clock.

She removed the wraps from her shoulders before the glass for a final view of herself in her glory. Suddenly she uttered a cry. Her necklace was not around her neck.

Her husband, already half undressed, asked: "What is the matter?"

She turned toward him excitedly:

"I have—I have—I no longer have Madame Forestier's necklace."

He arose in dismay: "What! How is that! Is not possible."

And they looked in the folds of the dress, in the folds of the mantle in the pockets, everywhere. They could not find it.

He asked: "You are sure you still had it when we left the house?"

"Yes, I felt it in the vestibule as we came out."

"But if you had lost it in the street we should have heard it fall. It must be in the cab."

"Yes. It is probable. Did you take the number?"

"No. And you, did you notice what it was?"

"No."

They looked at each other, utterly cast down. Finally Loisel dressed himself again.

"I am going," said he, "over the track where we went on foot, to see if I can find it."

And he went. She remained in her evening gown, not having the force to go to bed, stretched upon a chair, without ambition or thoughts.

Toward seven o'clock her husband returned. He had found nothing.

He went to the police and to the cab offices and put an advertisement in the newspapers, offering a reward; he did everything that afforded them a suspicion of hope.

She waited all day in a state of bewilderment before this frightful disaster. Loisel returned at evening, with his face harrowed and pale, and had discovered nothing.

"It will be necessary," said he, "to write to your friend that you have broken the clasp of the necklace and that you will have it repaired. That will give us time to turn around."

She wrote as he dictated.

At the end of a week they had lost all hope. And Loisel, older by five years, declared:

"We must take measures to replace this jewel."

The next day they took the box which had inclosed it to the jeweler whose name was on the inside. He consulted his books.

"It is not I, Madame," said he, "who sold this necklace; I only furnished the casket."

Then they went from jeweler to jeweler, seeking a necklace like the other one, consulting their memories, and ill, both of them, with chagrin and anxiety.

In a shop of the Palais-Royal they found a chaplet of diamonds which seemed to them exactly like the one they had lost. It was valued at forty thousand francs. They could get it for thirty-six thousand.

Stop reading at this point and assign students to write their own conclusion.

THE NECKLACE — concluded

GUY DE MAPASSANT

They begged the jeweler not to sell it for three days. And they made an arrangement by which they might return it for thirty-four thousand francs if they found the other one before the end of February.

Loisel possessed eighteen thousand francs which his father had left him.

He borrowed the rest.

He borrowed it, asking for a thousand francs of one, five hundred of another, five louis of this one and three louis of that one. He gave notes, made ruinous promises, took money of usurers and the whole race of lenders. He compromised his whole existence, in fact, risked his signature without even knowing whether he could make it good or not, and, harassed by anxiety for the future, by the black misery which surrounded him and by the prospect of all physical privations and moral torture, he went to get the new necklace, depositing on the merchant's counter thirty-six thousand francs.

When Mme Loisel took back the jewels to Mme Forestier the latter said to her in a frigid tone:

"You should have returned these to me sooner, for I might have needed them."

She did open the jewel box as her friend feared she would. If she should perceive the substitution what would she think? What should she say? Would she take her for a robber?

Mme Loisel now knew the horrible life of necessity. She did her part, however, completely, heroically. It was necessary to pay this frightful debt. She would pay it. They sent away the maid; they changed their lodgings they rented some rooms under a mansard roof.

She learned the heavy cares of a household, the odious work of a kitchen. She washed the dishes, using her rosy nails upon the greasy pots and the bottoms of the stewpans. She washed the soiled linen, the chemises and dishcloths, which she hung on the line to dry; she took down the refuse to the street each morning and brought up the water, stopping at each landing to breathe. And, clothed like a woman of the people, she went to the grocer's, the butcher's and the fruiterer's with her basket on her arm, shopping, haggling to the last sou her miserable money.

Every month it was necessary to renew some notes, thus obtaining time, and to pay others.

The husband worked evenings, putting the books of some merchants in order, and nights he often did copying at five sous a page.

And this life lasted for ten years.

At the end of ten years they had restored all, all, with interest of the usurer, and accumulated interest, besides.

Mme Loisel seemed old now. She had become a strong, hard woman, the crude woman of the poor household. Her hair badly dressed, her skirts awry, her hands red, she spoke in a loud tone and washed the floors in large pails of water. But sometimes, when her husband was at the office, she would sear herself before the window and think of that evening party of former times, of that ball where she was so beautiful and so flattered.

How would it have been if she had not lost that necklace? Who knows? Who knows? How singular is life and how full of changes! How small a thing will ruin or save one!

One Sunday, as she was taking a walk in the Champs Elysees to rid herself of the cares of the week, she suddenly perceived a woman walking with a child. It was Mme Forestier, still young, still pretty, still attractive. Mme Loisel was affected. Should she speak to her? Yes, certainly. And now that she had paid, she would tell her all. Why not?

She approached her. "Good morning, Jeanne."

Her friend did not recognize her and was astonished to be so familiarly addressed by this common personage. She stammered:

"But, Madame—I do not know—You must be mistaken."

"No, I am Matilda Loisel."

Her friend uttered a cry of astonishment: "Oh! my poor Matilda! How you have changed!"

"Yes, I have had some hard days since I saw you, and some miserable ones—and all because of you."

© Substitute Teacher Training Institute

THE NECKLACE — concluded

GUY DE MAPASSANT

"Because of me? How is that?"

"You recall the diamond necklace that you loaned me to wear to the minister's ball?"

"Yes, very well."

"Well, I lost it."

"How is that, since you returned it to me?"

"I returned another to you exactly like it. And it has taken us ten years to pay for it. You can understand that it was not easy for us who have nothing. But it is finished, and I am decently content."

Mme Forestier stopped short. She said:

"You say that you bought a diamond necklace to replace mine?"

"Yes. You did not perceive it then? They were just alike."

And she smiled with a proud and simple joy. Mme Forestier was touched and took both her hands as she replied:

"Oh, my poor Matilda! Mine were false. They were not worth over five hundred francs!"

Masterpieces of Literature

Great works of literature have been produced in a number of forms: poetry, drama, fiction, and essay. Try to match the titles below with a description and author of the literary work.

_____ 1. Anti-Utopian novel by George Orwell written in the form of a beast fable. A group of animals overthrow their human masters and set up a communal society.

_____ 2. A collection of tales, mostly in verse, by Geoffrey Chaucer. They tell of the poet joining a company of pilgrims on their way to visit the shrine of St. Thomas `a Becket.

_____ 3. The disenchantment with a hostile adult world, of a young runaway in New York written by J.D. Salinger.

_____ 4. Written by Feodor Dostoevski, this novel develops the theme of redemption through suffering, in the life of a penniless student who commits murder.

_____ 5. A play written by Arthur Miller about the modern tragedy of an ordinary, aging, American man, who eventually puts an end to his own life.

_____ 6. Novels of early frontier life written by James Fennimore Cooper. All stories feature Natty Bumppo as the hero.

_____ 7. A novel written by F. Scott Fitzgerald whose violent plot exposes the thoughtless cruelty of great wealth.

_____ 8. A Shakespearean play in which Egeus, father of Hermia, promises her to Demetrius despite her love for Lysander.

_____ 9. Jane Austen's book set in the English countryside which concerns the Bennett family's attempts to find suitable husbands for three daughters.

_____ 10. A somber tale of love and vengeance written by Emily Bronte. Lead by thwarted love its central character takes revenge on the woman he loves and her family.

_____ 11. A play authored by Tennessee Williams in which an aging unstable Southern belle comes to stay with her sister in the French Quarter of New Orleans.

_____ 12. The story of Captain Ahab's search for the great white whale that crippled him, written by Herman Melville.

_____ 13. A trilogy of fantasy novels written by J.R.R. Tolkien, about the often grim and sometimes terrible quest of the Hobbits.

_____ 14. Written by Thornton Wilder, this play deals with the cycle of life in Grovers Corners. A narrator comments about the town's activities and leading citizens.

© Substitute Teacher Training Institute

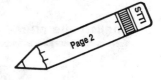

Masterpieces of Literature

_____ 15. Classic stories of small-town American boyhood based on Mark Twain's memories of growing up in Hannibal, Missouri.

_____ 16. Homer's epic of the king of Ithica's ten year voyage home from war. An account of his wanderings and hardships.

_____ 17. Written by Leo Tolstoy, this epic novel provides a view of Russian society in the beginning of the 19th century.

_____ 18. A melodramatic tale of poverty and the London underworld, written by British author Charles Dickens.

_____ 19. A study of a man's feelings in battle, written by Stephen Crane. One of the first books to treat battle realistically, rather than as a backdrop for gallantry.

_____ 20. A satire written by Jonathan Swift, that tells the tales of a man's voyages to imaginary lands.

A. Moby Dick

B. Crime and Punishment

C. Death of a Salesman

D. War and Peace

E. Odyssey

F. Animal Farm

G. The Red Badge of Courage

H. Gulliver's Travels

I. Our Town

J. Wuthering Heights

K. The Adventures of Tom Sawyer

L. A Streetcar Named Desire

M. Pride and Prejudice

N. Oliver Twist

O. The Lord of the Rings

P. Leatherstocking Tales

Q. The Great Gatsby

R. Catcher in the Rye

S. The Canterbury Tales

T. A Midsummer Night's Dream

Masterpieces of Literature ANSWER KEY

1.	F	Animal Farm
2.	S	The Canterbury Tales
3.	R	Catcher in the Rye
4.	B	Crime and Punishment
5.	C	Death of a Salesman
6.	P	Leatherstocking Tales
7.	Q	The Great Gatsby
8.	T	A Midsummer Night's Dream
9.	M	Pride and Prejudice
10.	J	Wuthering Heights
11.	L	A Streetcar Named Desire
12.	A	Moby Dick
13.	O	Lord of the Rings
14.	I	Our Town
15.	K	The Adventures of Tom Sawyer
16.	E	Odyssey
17.	D	War and Peace
18.	N	Oliver Twist
19.	G	Red Badge of Courage
20.	H	Gulliver's Travels

© Substitute Teacher Training Institute

Fill in the _____

Complete the following phrases, then write your interpretation of the phrase on the back of this paper.

1. The early bird catches the _____

2. Early to bed early to rise makes a man healthy wealthy and _____

3. A penny for your _____

4. The hand that rocks the cradle rules the _____

5. Don't put all of your eggs in one _____

6. Never count your chickens before they _____

7. Beggars can't be _____

8. A bird in the hand is worth two in the _____

9. Haste makes _____

10. The straw that broke the camel's _____

11. Many hands make light _____

12. His bark is worse than his _____

13. When the cat's away, the mice will _____

14. Two heads are better than _____

15. An old dog can't be taught new _____

16. Putting the cart before the _____

17. As easy as falling off a _____

18. Letting the cat out of the _____

19. There is no honor among _____

20. Barking up the wrong _____

Fill in the Blank ANSWER KEY

1. The early bird catches the worm.

2. Early to bed early to rise makes a man healthy wealthy and wise.

3. A penny for your thoughts.

4. The hand that rocks the cradle rules the world.

5. Don't put all of your eggs in one basket.

6. Never count your chickens before they hatch.

7. Beggars can't be choosers.

8. A bird in the hand is worth two in the bush.

9. Haste makes waste.

10. The straw that broke the camel's back.

11. Many hands make light work.

12. His bark is worse than his bite.

13. When the cat's away, the mice will play.

14. Two heads are better than one.

15. An old dog can't be taught new tricks.

16. Putting the cart before the horse.

17. As easy as falling off a log.

18. Letting the cat out of the bag.

19. There is no honor among thieves.

20. Barking up the wrong tree.

Literature Terminology

Listed below are 25 terms associated with the study of literature. Can you match each one with the correct definition?

_____ 1.   comedy

_____ 2.   anonymous

_____ 3.   edit

_____ 4.   essay

_____ 5.   folklore

_____ 6.   novel

_____ 7.   pseudonym

_____ 8.   plagiarism

_____ 9.   play

_____ 10. fiction

_____ 11. refrain

_____ 12. short story

_____ 13. tragedy

_____ 14. trilogy

_____ 15. sonnet

_____ 16. verse

_____ 17. title page

_____ 18. playwright

_____ 19. hero

_____ 20. review

_____ 21. publish

_____ 22. translate

_____ 23. heroine

_____ 24. revision

_____ 25. character

A.   the page of a book showing the author and title

B.   a poem in fourteen lines following strict rules

C.   the principal female character in a literary work

D.   to change or refine a writer's work

E.   giving no name as the author of a work

F.   a story meant to be performed by actors on a stage

G.   a brief work of fiction in prose

H.   a brief prose which addresses a particular subject

I.   the result of rewriting a work in an effort to improve it

J.   long work of fiction in prose (not poetry)

K.   legends passed from one generation to another

L.   to steal or pass off another's work as your own

M.   a pen name or invented name used by a writer

N.   an invented story

O.   a line or lines repeated during a poem

P.   a literary work intended to amuse

Q.   to produce a print version of a literary work

R.   a serious work with an unhappy ending

S.   a person in a literary work

T.   an evaluation of a literary work

U.   someone who writes plays

V.   the principal male character in a literary work

W.   to turn a work into another language

X.   lines of rhymed or rhythmic writing

Y.   a series of three related works

Literature Terminology ANSWER KEY

1. comedy — P. a literary work intended to amuse
2. anonymous — E. giving no name as the author of a work
3. edit — D. to change or refine a writer's work
4. essay — H. brief prose addressing a particular subject
5. folklore — K. legends passed from one generation to another
6. novel — J. a long work of fiction in prose (not poetry)
7. pseudonym — M. a pen name or invented name used by a writer
8. plagiarism — L. to steal or pass off another's work as your own
9. play — F. a story meant to be performed by actors on a stage
10. fiction — N. an invented story
11. refrain — O. a line or lines repeated during a poem
12. short story — G. a brief work of fiction in prose
13. tragedy — R. a serious work with an unhappy ending
14. trilogy — Y. a series of three related works
15. sonnet — B. a poem in fourteen lines following strict rules
16. verse — X. lines of rhymed or rhythmic writing
17. title page — A. the page of a book showing the author and title
18. playwright — U. someone who writes plays
19. hero — V. the principal male character in a literary work
20. review — T. an evaluation of a literary work
21. publish — Q. to produce a print version of a literary work
22. translate — W. to turn a work into another language
23. heroine — C. the principal female character in a literary work
24. revision — I. the result of rewriting a work in an effort to improve it
25. character — S. a person in a literary work

© Substitute Teacher Training Institute

Author Trivia

You probably recognize the names of the authors listed below. But can you match the author to one of their well known works and an event or characteristic of their life? Write the number from the title of the book they authored and the letter from the trivia about their life, in the blanks before their name.

Author	Title	Trivia
_____ _____ Miguel De Cervantes	1. Pride and Prejudice	A. She loved to dance and one year wore through four pair of dancing slippers.
_____ _____ William Shakespeare	2. The Ugly Duckling	B. As a boy he liked to shock people by pulling a sheet over his head and coming into the room like a ghost.
_____ _____ Jane Austen	3. The Secret Garden	C. She worked as an army nurse during the Civil War until she fell ill with typhoid pneumonia.
_____ _____ Hans Christian Anderson	4. The Raven	D. He and his relatives were once thrown in jail after neighbors wrongly accused them of involvement in a local murder.
_____ _____ Edgar Allan Poe	5. Tom Sawyer	E. He often worried that he was going blind and wore a green eye shade when he was working.
_____ _____ Charles Dickens	6. Hamlet	F. Though he made almost no money from his writing he did earn a modest fortune as an actor which he invested in real estate.
_____ _____ Emily Bronte	7. Little Women	G. At school he wrote stories on scraps of paper and sold them to schoolmates for marbles.
_____ _____ Emily Dickinson	8. Don Quixote	H. She liked to furnish doll houses; the last one she owned had a working shower.
_____ _____ Louisa May Alcott	9. A Tale of Two Cities	I. As a young man he sold roach powder, played the piano and drove a Model T Ford across the country.
_____ _____ Mark Twain	10. Because I could not stop for Death	J. He was afraid of death and sometimes put a sign next to his bed that read I AM NOT REALLY DEAD so that people would know he was just asleep.

Author Trivia

_____ _____ Frances Hodgson Burnett

_____ _____ Robert Louis Stevenson

_____ _____ Jack London

_____ _____ Carl Sandburg

_____ _____ E. B. White

11. Charlotte's Web

12. Wuthering Heights

13. White Fang

14. Treasure Island

15. Chicago

K. He reminded many people of a Greek god, with his tanned face, strong neck and eyes that seemed to change color.

L. After catching cold at her brother's funeral she never recovered and refused treatment until two hours before her death.

M. She described the dictionary as her "only companion" and books as "the strongest friend."

N. Whenever he went bankrupt, he would go on another lecture tour to make his money back.

O. He did most of his writing propped up in bed wearing a red flannel dressing gown with a pad of paper across his knees.

© Substitute Teacher Training Institute

Answers

Author Trivia ANSWER KEY

		Author	Title	Trivia
8	D	Miguel De Cervantes	Don Quixote	He and his relatives were once thrown in jail after neighbors wrongly accused them of involvement in a local murder.
6	F	William Shakespeare	Hamlet	Though he made almost no money from his writing he did earn a modest fortune as an actor which he invested in real estate.
1	A	Jane Austen	Pride and Prejudice	She loved to dance and one year wore through four pair of dancing slippers.
2	J	Hans Christian Anderson	The Ugly Duckling	He was afraid of death and sometimes put a sign next to his bed that read I AM NOT REALLY DEAD so that people would know he was just asleep.
4	B	Edgar Allan Poe	The Raven	As a boy he liked to shock people by pulling a sheet over his head and coming into the room like a ghost.
9	G	Charles Dickens	A Tale of Two Cities	At school he wrote stories on scraps of paper and sold them to schoolmates for marbles.
12	L	Emily Bronte	Wuthering Heights	After catching cold at her brother's funeral she never recovered and refused treatment until two hours before her death.
10	M	Emily Dickinson	Because I could not stop for Death	She described the dictionary as her "only companion" and books as "the strongest friend."
7	C	Louisa May Alcott	Little Women	She worked as an army nurse during the Civil War until she fell ill with typhoid pneumonia.

5	N	Mark Twain	Tom Sawyer	Whenever he went bankrupt, he would go on another lecture tour to make his money back.
3	H	Frances Hodgson Burnett	The Secret Garden	She liked to furnish doll houses; the last one she owned had a working shower.
14	O	Robert Louis Stevenson	Treasure Island	He did most of his writing propped up in bed wearing a red flannel dressing gown with a pad of paper across his knees.
14	K	Jack London	White Fang	He reminded many people of a Greek god, with his tanned face, strong neck and eyes that seemed to change color.
15	E	Carl Sandburg	Chicago	He often worried that he was going blind and wore a green eye shade when he was working.
11	I	E. B. White	Charlotte's Web	As a young man he sold roach powder, played the piano and drove a Model T Ford across the country.

© Substitute Teacher Training Institute

Foreign Sponges

Similar to the sponge activities in the general interest section at the beginning of this chapter, the following sponge activities have been adapted to challenge student foreign language skills. Whenever possible, have students write or speak their responses in the language they are studying.

1. Name as many cities as you can where _____ (language) is spoken.

2. List as many colors as you can.

3. Write the names of the months and days of the week.

4. List the numbers from one to one hundred.

5. Write the alphabet.

7. Describe what you are wearing.

8. List 15 objects you can see from where you are sitting.

9. Write down the names of all of the holidays you know.

10. Suppose a friend who doesn't speak _____ (language) was going on vacation to _____ (country where language is spoken), what would be the 10 most useful words you think they should learn before leaving.

- -

Slapstick

Arrange student desks in a circle. Each student is assigned a word in the language they are studying (recent vocabulary lists work great). One student is selected to stand in the center of the circle with a rolled up newspaper. The teacher calls out one of the assigned words and the student to whom the word has been assigned must quickly call out another word before the student in the center can "slap" their desk with the newspaper. Play continues until someone doesn't say a word before having their desk slapped, or mispronounces a word. In either event the student assumes the role of the person in the center, who returns to their desk. Play resumes until class is over or students lose interest.

In large classes it may be beneficial to create two circles, thus allowing for more student involvement and interaction. Changing the assigned words halfway through the class will help to keep things interesting and challenging.

An Object Lesson

Time: 30 minutes +

Objective: Students will match foreign language labels with common classroom objects.

Materials: foreign language labels, sack, tape

Advance Preparation: Copy and cut apart the appropriate labels for the language being taught.

Procedure:

1.   Place labels in the bag.

2.   Have students come to the front of the room, draw a label from the bag, pronounce the word on the label, and tape it to the corresponding object in the classroom.

3.   Repeat step two until all students have had a turn.

4.   Correct the students' work by removing incorrect labels and asking for volunteers to try and place them where they should be. Repeat this process until all labels are correctly matched with the corresponding objects.

If time permits students may enjoy trying to complete the same activity with labels in another language.

            © Substitute Teacher Training Institute

ANSWER KEY

	Classroom Object	Spanish	French	German
1.	book	libro	Livre	das Buch
2.	paper	papel	Papier	das Papier
3.	desk	escritorio	Pupitre	das Pult
4.	floor	suelo	Plancher	der Boden
5.	chair	silla	Chaise	der Stuhl
6.	flag	bandera	Pendre mollement	die Fahne
7.	pencil	lápiz	Crayon	der Bleistift
8.	pen	pluma	plume	die Feder
9.	wall	pared	Muraille	die Wand
10.	light switch	luz	Lumière	das Licht
11.	door	puerta	Porte	die Tür
12.	door handle	tirador	Pignée de porte	die Türknopf
13.	window	ventana	Fenêtre	das Fenster
14.	poster	cartel	Affiche	das Plakat
15.	heater	calentador	Personne quie chauffe	der Heizkörper
16.	thermostat	termostado	Thermostat	der Thermostat
17.	shoe	zapato	Soulier	der Schuh
18.	computer	ordenador	Machine á calculer	der Kalkulator
19.	plant	planta	Plante	der Pflanze
20.	book shelf	estante	Rayon	das Bücherbord
21.	box	caja	Boîte	der Buchsbarn
22.	scissors	tijeras	ciseaux	mit der Schere
23.	tape	cinta	Ruban	das Leukoplast
24.	pencil sharpener	tajalápiz	Taille-crayon	der Bleistiftspitzer
25.	stapler	grapadora	Agrafeuse	der Sortierer
25.	paper clips	grapa	Attache	die Heftklammer
26.	closet	armario	Cabinet	das Kabinett
27.	writing	palabra	Mot	das Wort
28.	assignment	asignación	Attribution	die Zuweisung
29.	electricity	electricidad	Électricité	Elektrizität

Spanish	French	German
libro	Livre	das Buch
papel	Papier	das Papier
escritorio	Pupitre	das Pult
suelo	Plancher	.der Boden
silla	Chaise	der Stuhl
bandera	Pendre mollement	die Fahne
lápiz	Crayon	der Bleistift
pluma	plume	die Feder
pared	Muraille	die Wand
luz	Lumière	das Licht
puerta	Porte	die Tür

tirador	Poignée de porte	die Türknopf
ventana	Fenêtre	das Fenster
cartel	Affiche	das Plakat
calentador	Personne quie chauffe	der Heizkörper
termostado	Thermostat	der Thermostat
zapato	Soulier	der Schuh
ordenador	Machine á calculer	der Kalkulator
planta	Plante	der Pflanze
estante	Rayon	das Bücherbord
caja	Boîte	der Buchsbarn
tijeras	ciseaux	mit der Schere
cinta	Ruban	das Leukoplast

tajalápiz	Taille-crayon	der Bleistiftspitzer
grapadora	Agrafeuse	der Sortierer
grapa	Attache	die Heftklammer
armario	Cabinet	das Kabinett
palabra	Mot	das Wort
asignación	Attribution	die Zuweisung
electricidad	Électricité	Elektrizität

© Substitute Teacher Training Institute

Greetings in any Language

Time: 30 minutes

Objective: Students will create a greeting card with text written in a foreign language.

Materials: plain paper, pencils

Optional Materials: colored paper, markers, colored pencils, stencils, scissors, glue, samples of commercial greeting cards, etc.

Advance Preparation: Assemble needed materials.

Procedure:

1. Assign students to create a greeting card with text written in the foreign language they are studying. The theme of the card may be assigned by the teacher or decided individually by the students. Theme ideas are listed below.

2. Encourage students to enhance the text with creative artwork.

3. Distribute paper and art supplies.

4. Monitor student work as they complete the assignment.

Greeting Card Themes:

Holiday

Get Well

Good Luck

Birthday

Thinking of You

Congratulations

Picture That

Time: 30 minutes +

Objective: Students will write a newspaper article in a foreign language.

Materials: large picture (poster size) for class display or individual pictures for students, pencils, paper

Advance Preparation: Select and prepare picture(s) for in-class use.

Procedure:

1.   Distribute or display pictures*.

2.   Explain to students that they are to write (in the language they are studying) a newspaper paper article which correlates with the picture.

3.   Set a time limit for completion.

4.   Monitor student work.

5.   If time permits, have volunteers share their articles either with the whole class or in small groups.

6.   Have students turn in articles and pictures for teacher evaluation.

*Pictures cut from magazines, mounted on construction paper, and laminated or placed in clear plastic sleeves work well for repeated use throughout the school year.

Spanish Translate / Eliminate

One of the words in each group below does not belong. Translate the words, then cross out the one that does not belong. An example has been completed for you.

Example:

coche	tren	avion	~~ordenador~~
car	train	airplane	computer

1.	bizcocho	pastel	hielo	empanada
2.	zoológico	cocina	dormitorio	cuarto de baño
3.	nube	hierba	estrella	luna
4.	libro	teléfono	periódico	revista
5.	tijeras	cuchillo	tenedor	cuchara
6.	caballo	intimidar	gato	flor
7.	falda	camisa	paraguas	calcetín
8.	agua	plátano	leche	zumo
9.	hombre	casa	árbol	pez
10.	televisión	radio	dinero	ordenador
11.	serpiente	rana	pájaro	roca
12.	búho	escritorio	estudiante	silla
13.	lápiz	papel	pastel	pluma
14.	concha	agua	regla	arena
15.	pie	boca	nariz	oreja

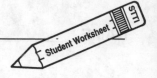

French Translate / Eliminate

One of the words in each group below does not belong. Translate the words then cross out the one that does not belong.

Example:

| char | suite | aeroplane | ~~machine á claculer~~ |
| car | train | airplane | computer |

1.	petit pain au lait	gâteau	glace	pâté
2.	jardin zoologique	cuisine	chambre á coucher	salle de bain
3.	nuage	herbe	étoile	lune
4.	livre	téléphone	journal	magasin
5.	ciseaux	couteau	fourchette	cuiller
6.	cheval	vache	chat	fleur
7.	jupe	chemise	parapluie	chaussette
8.	eau	banane	lait	jus
9.	personne	maison	arbre	poisson
10.	télévision	télégraphie sans fil	argent	machine é calculer
11.	serpent	grenouille	diseau	rocher
12.	hibou	pupitre	étudiant	chaise
13.	crayon	papier	pastel	plume
14.	coquillage	eua	règle	sable
15.	pied	bouche	nez	oreille

© Substitute Teacher Training Institute

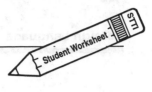

German Translate / Eliminate

One of the words in each group below does not belong. Translate the words, then cross out the one
that does not belong. An example has been completed for you.

Example:

der Kraft	die Schleppe	die Luft	der Kalkulator
car (wagon)	train	airplane	computer

1. Schiffsküche   der Kuchen   das Eis   die Pastete

2. der Zoo   die Kuche   das Schlafzimmer   die Toilette

3. die Wolke   das Gras   der Stern   der Mond

4. das Buch   der Fernspreacher die Zeitung   das Magazin

5. mit der Schere   das Messer   die Gabel   der Löffel

6. das Pferd   die Kuh   die Katze   die Blume

7. der Rock   das Hemd   der Schirm   die Socke

8. das Wasser   die Banane   die Milch   der Saft

9. der Mann   das Haus   der Baum   der Fisch

10. das Fernsehen   das Radio   das Geld   der Kalkulator

11. die Schlange   der Schnurbesatz   der Vogel   der Fels

12. die Eule   das Pult   der Student   der Stuhl

13. der Bleistift   das Papier   der Farbstift   die Feder

14. die Muschel   das Wasser   der Herrscher   der Sand

15. der Fuß   der Mund   die Nase   das Ohr

Translate / Eliminate Answer Key

EXAMPLE:

	car	train	airplane	~~computer~~
1.	cookies	cake	~~ice~~	pie
2.	~~zoo~~	kitchen	bedroom	bathroom
3.	clouds	~~grass~~	stars	moon
4.	book	~~telephone~~	newspaper	magazine
5.	~~scissors~~	knife	fork	spoon
6.	horse	cow	cat	~~flower~~
7.	skirt	shirt	~~umbrella~~	sock
8.	water	~~banana~~	milk	juice
9.	man	~~house~~	tree	fish
10.	television	radio	~~money~~	computer
11.	snake	frog	bird	~~rock~~
12.	~~owl~~	desk	student	chair
13.	pencil	~~paper~~	crayon	pen
14.	shell	water	~~ruler~~	sand
15.	~~foot~~	mouth	nose	ear

© Substitute Teacher Training Institute

More Language Activities

1. Make a crossword puzzle in French, Spanish, German, Latin, or another foreign language you are studying. The clues may be in English.

2. Make a crossword puzzle in the language you are studying. The clues must be in the same language.

3. Draw the floor plan of a house. Label the rooms, doors, windows, and furniture in Spanish, French, German, or any other non-English language.

4. Play a game of "buzz", speaking only German, Spanish, or French. The first person calls out the word for "one" the second, "two"; the third "three"; and so on around the room. Every time a number that contains seven or is a multiple of seven (i.e., 7, 14, 17, 21) comes up call out "buzz" instead of the number. Remember, 'buzz' is the only English word allowed!

5. Play a game of telephone, using only the language you are studying. The first person chooses a phrase or sentence in Spanish, French, or German and whispers it to the person next to him. That person, without asking him to repeat it, whispers the same phrase, as he understands it, to the next person, and so on. The last person in the row says the phrase out loud and translates it into English.

6. Make a calendar for this month, using only the foreign language you are studying. No abbreviations are permitted.

7. Play twenty questions. One student chooses an object and tells the class whether it is animal, vegetable, or mineral. The rest of the class takes turns asking him questions that can be answered only "yes" or "no" until they guess the subject, or until they have asked twenty questions and still can't guess. Both the object and the questions must be stated in the foreign language the class is studying.

8. Play "stump the experts". Three students volunteer or are chosen as experts. Members of the class take turns giving them words in the foreign language for one of the experts to translate into English. If he can do it, he remains as expert. If he can't, the one who stumped him becomes the expert. Later, class members give words in English and the experts translate it into the language being studied.

9. In the language you are studying, write directions explaining step-by-step how to do a simple task, such as putting on a hat and coat, cooking an egg, or sawing a board. Select a volunteer and without telling him what the task is or using any English, read your directions to him and have him carry out the instructions.

10. Write a limerick in the language you are studying. Remember, the first, second, and fifth lines rhyme and the third and fourth lines rhyme.

11. Select one student as moderator and hold a spelling bee entirely in the language you are studying. Use words in the foreign language text used by the class.

12. Select one student as moderator and hold a vocabulary bee. The moderator, using the foreign language text, gives words in English. Students must translate the words.

13. In English, write a description of a major country where the language you are studying is spoken. Include any small details you may know.

14. Arrange a display of several items from around the room on a desk while a volunteer is out of the room. Have him come in and study the display for one minute, then, without looking at it again, list everything on the desk from memory. The student must use the language being studied.

15. Play "concentration". Divide into teams of two. Cut paper into 3-by-5-inch pieces and make a set of concentration cards, using antonyms in the language you are studying. For instance, if Spanish is your language, one card might read "si", its match would be "no", one card might read "noche", its match "dia", one card might read "caliente", its match "frio", and so on. Make ten to twenty pairs.

    To play, spread out all the cards, face down. The first player turns over any two cards and shows them to the other player. If they should be a matching pair of antonyms, he then puts them face up at his side of the table. The first player may then have another try at finding a matched pair. If the first player does not find a match, the second player tries to remember where and what has been turned up and attempts to find a matched pair. Both players must see the cards turned up each time to help them locate matches. The game continues until the last card has been picked up. One point is given for each matched pair. The high score wins.

© Substitute Teacher Training Institute

16. Play a traveling game; each student must think of some item to go in a suitcase, using only the language being studied. The first person in the first row must pack something beginning with the letter "a", the second with "b", the third must start with "c", and so on. Ready? "I am going to visit relatives, so I will get out my big suitcase and pack it with my..."

    Examples in Spanish:

    > First student—"Abrigos"

    > Second student—"Botas"

    If a student makes a correct addition—it doesn't need to be a sensible one—he earns one point. If he cannot think of one, he loses two points.

17. Play super sentence. Let one student choose ten or twelve words from the dictionary in the language being studied and write them on the board. In ten minutes, the rest of the class tries to write a sentence using all the words or as many as they can. Read the sentence aloud.

You Are Here

Time: 30 minutes +

Objective: Students will identify specific locations on a map.

Materials: a large map of the world, a continent, or country (many classrooms will be equipped with a roll-down map mounted on the wall, other wise a folding paper map can be taped to a wall), prizes for the winning team

Advance preparation: If you are unfamiliar with locations on the map to be used, make a list of at least 30 different: towns, rivers, cities, etc., that can be identified on the map.

Procedure:

1.   Divide the class into two teams.

2.   Have one person from each team come and stand in front of the map.

3.   Begin the activity by saying, " I am in _____(city, state or other identifiable location on the map). Where am I?"

4.   Students then compete to be the first one to locate and point to the location on the map.

5.   Award one point to the team who located the designated spot first, while students return to their desk.

6.   Have a different student from each team stand in front of the map.

7.   Repeat steps three through six until every student has had a turn, class is over, or students lose interest.

8.   Award a prize to the winning team.

© Substitute Teacher Training Institute

NAME _____

State Nicknames

Every state in the United States has a nickname. How many states can you correctly match with their nicknames.

	State		Nickname
_____1.	Alaska	A.	Palmetto State
_____2.	Arizona	B.	The First State or Diamond State
_____3.	Arkansas	C.	Empire State of the South or Peach State
_____4.	California	D.	Show Me State
_____5.	Colorado	E.	Peace Garden State
_____6.	Connecticut	F.	Badger State
_____7.	Delaware	G.	The Last Frontier
_____8.	Florida	H.	The Sunflower State
_____9.	Georgia	I.	Green Mountain State
_____10.	Hawaii	J.	Garden State
_____11.	Idaho	K.	Sooner State
_____12.	Illinois	L.	Volunteer State
_____13.	Indiana	M.	Old Line State or Free State
_____14.	Iowa	N.	The Prairie State
_____15.	Kansas	O.	The Pelican State
_____16.	Kentucky	P.	The Golden State
_____17.	Louisiana	Q.	Sage Brush State or Silver State
_____18.	Maine	R.	Old Dominion
_____19.	Maryland	S.	The District
_____20.	Massachusetts	T.	Keystone State
_____21.	Michigan	U.	Tar Heel State or Old North State
_____22.	Minnesota	V.	The Grand Canyon State
_____23.	Mississippi	W.	The Centennial State
_____24.	Missouri	X.	The Gem State
_____25.	Montana	Y.	North Star State or Gopher State
_____26.	Nebraska	Z.	Cornhusker State

State Nicknames

_____ 27.	Nevada	AA.	Granite State
_____ 28.	New Hampshire	BB.	Equality State
_____ 29.	New Jersey	CC.	The Evergreen State
_____ 30.	New Mexico	DD.	Beaver State
_____ 31.	New York	EE.	The Bay State or Old Colony
_____ 32.	North Carolina	FF.	The Hawkeye State
_____ 33.	North Dakota	GG.	The Sunshine State
_____ 34.	Ohio	HH.	The Constitution State or Nutmeg State
_____ 35.	Oklahoma	II.	Lone Star State
_____ 36.	Oregon	JJ.	The Blue Grass State
_____ 37.	Pennsylvania	KK.	Mountain State
_____ 38.	Rhode Island	LL.	Beehive State
_____ 39.	South Carolina	MM.	The Empire State
_____ 40.	South Dakota	NN.	Treasure State
_____ 41.	Tennessee	OO.	Little Rhody or Ocean State
_____ 42.	Texas	PP.	The Aloha State
_____ 43.	Utah	QQ.	The Land of Opportunity
_____ 44.	Vermont	RR.	The Pine Tree State
_____ 45.	Virginia	SS.	Mount Rushmore State or Coyote State
_____ 46.	Washington	TT.	Buckeye State
_____ 47.	West Virginia	UU.	The Land of Enchantment
_____ 48.	Wisconsin	VV.	Magnolia State
_____ 49.	Wyoming	WW.	The Great Lakes State or Wolverine State
_____ 50.	District of Columbia	XX.	The Hoosier State

© Substitute Teacher Training Institute

Answers

State Nicknames ANSWER KEY

	State		Nickname
1.	Alaska	G.	The Last Frontier
2.	Arizona	V.	The Grand Canyon State
3.	Arkansas	QQ.	The Land of Opportunity
4.	California	P.	The Golden State
5.	Colorado	W.	The Centennial State
6.	Connecticut	HH.	The Constitution State or Nutmeg State
7.	Delaware	B.	The First State or Diamond State
8.	Florida	GG.	The Sunshine State
9.	Georgia	C.	Empire State of the South or Peach State
10.	Hawaii	PP.	The Aloha State
11.	Idaho	X.	The Gem State
12.	Illinois	N.	The Prairie State
13.	Indiana	XX.	The Hoosier State
14.	Iowa	FF.	The Hawkeye State
15.	Kansas	H.	The Sunflower State
16.	Kentucky	JJ.	The Blue Grass State
17.	Louisiana	O.	The Pelican State
18.	Maine	RR.	The Pine Tree State
19.	Maryland	M.	Old Line State or Free State
20.	Massachusetts	EE.	The Bay State or Old Colony
21.	Michigan	WW.	The Great Lakes State or Wolverine State
22.	Minnesota	Y.	North Star State or Gopher State
23.	Mississippi	VV.	Magnolia State
24.	Missouri	D.	Show Me State
25.	Montana	NN.	Treasure State
26.	Nebraska	Z.	Cornhusker State

Answers

State Nicknames ANSWER KEY (Continued)

27.	Nevada	Q.	Sage Brush State or Silver State
28.	New Hampshire	AA.	Granite State
29.	New Jersey	J.	Garden State
30.	New Mexico	UU.	The Land of Enchantment
31.	New York	MM.	The Empire State
32.	North Carolina	U.	Tar Heel State or Old North State
33.	North Dakota	E.	Peace Garden State
34.	Ohio	TT.	Buckeye State
35.	Oklahoma	K.	Sooner State
36.	Oregon	DD.	Beaver State
37.	Pennsylvania	T.	Keystone State
38.	Rhode Island	OO.	Little Rhody or Ocean State
39.	South Carolina	A.	Palmetto State
40.	South Dakota	SS.	Mount Rushmore State or Coyote State
41.	Tennessee	L.	Volunteer State
42.	Texas	II.	Lone Star State
43.	Utah	LL.	Beehive State
44.	Vermont	I.	Green Mountain State
45.	Virginia	R.	Old Dominion
46.	Washington	CC.	The Evergreen State
47.	West Virginia	KK.	Mountain State
48.	Wisconsin	F.	Badger State
49.	Wyoming	BB.	Equality State
50.	District of Columbia	S.	The District

© Substitute Teacher Training Institute

Locations and Associations

Activity One: Locating the States

Use the list of states below to locate and correctly label as many states as you can on the blank map. Do not "cross-out" the states on the list. You will use the list again in activity two. Use a map to check your work.

Alabama	Nebraska
Alaska	Nevada
Arizona	New Hampshire
Arkansas	New Jersey
California	New Mexico
Colorado	New York
Connecticut	North Carolina
Delaware	North Dakota
Florida	Ohio
Georgia	Oklahoma
Hawaii	Oregon
Idaho	Pennsylvania
Illinois	Rhode Island
Indiana	South Carolina
Iowa	South Dakota
Kansas	Tennessee
Kentucky	Texas
Louisiana	Utah
Maine	Vermont
Maryland	Virginia
Massachusetts	Washington
Michigan	West Virginia
Minnesota	Wisconsin
Mississippi	Wyoming
Missouri	District of Columbia
Montana	

Activity Two: State Associations

Next to each state on the list in activity one, write down one or two words which you associate with that state. For example you might associate "orange juice" with the state of Florida or "igloos" with the state of Alaska.

When you have finished, share your association words with a partner while they try and guess which state you are referring to. Then switch roles and you try to guess the states from their associations.

Page 2

LLTS

Word Topography

Topography is a term which relates the shape of something. In geography a topographical map is one which illustrates the land formations of the area. Use your topographical skills to match the geographical terms below to the word shapes on the right. Then turn your paper over and correctly use each word in a sentence.

1. scale

2. precipitation

3. vegetation

4. boundary

5. continent

6. degree

7. tundra   s c a l e

8. symbol

9. latitude

10. hemisphere

11. elevation

12. climate

13. country

14. topographical

15. equator

Where in the World

Listed below are 10 famous events and 10 well known places. Fill in the blanks as accurately and completely as you can.

Where did it happen?

1. Writing of the Declaration of Independence _____

2. First Olympics held _____

3. Abraham Lincoln died _____

4. Columbus first landed _____

5. Treaty of Versailles signed _____

6. Custer's Last Stand _____

7. President John F. Kennedy assassinated _____

8. Surrender papers of the Civil War signed _____

9. Wright brothers first airplane flight _____

10. Martin Luther King shot and killed _____

Where is it at?

1. Westminster Abbey _____

2. Grand Canyon _____

3. Louvre _____

4. Taj Mahal _____

5. Pyramids _____

6. Rodeo Drive _____

7. Leaning Tower of Pisa _____

8. Mount Rushmore _____

9. Eiffel Tower _____

10. Statue of Liberty _____

© Substitute Teacher Training Institute

Where in the World ANSWER KEY

Where did it happen?

1. Writing of the Declaration of Independence — Philadelphia , PA

2. First Olympics held — Olympia in Southern Greece (776 BC)

3. Abraham Lincoln died — Peterson Boarding House across the street from Ford's Theater in Washington DC

4. Columbus first landed — a small island in the Bahamas

5. Treaty of Versailles signed — Versailles, France (a suburb of Paris)

6. Custer's Last Stand — Indian encampment along the Little Big Horn River in Montana

7. President John F. Kennedy assassinated — Dallas, TX

8. Surrender papers of the Civil War signed — Mclean House near the Appomattox Courthouse in Appomattox, VA

9. Wright brothers first airplane flight — Kitty Hawk, NC

10. Martin Luther King shot and killed — balcony of the Lorraine Motel in Memphis, TN

Where is it at?

1. Westminster Abbey — London, England

2. Grand Canyon — Arizona

3. Louvre — Paris, France

4. Taj Mahal — Agra, India

5. Pyramids — four miles south of Cairo, Egypt

6. Rodeo Drive — Beverly Hills, CA

7. Leaning Tower of Pisa — Pisa, Italy

8. Mount Rushmore — South Dakota

9. Eiffel Tower — Paris, France

10. Statue of Liberty — Ellis Island, geographically a part of New Jersey but thought of as belonging to New York

Supreme Court Cases

Time: 30+ minutes

Objective: Students will discuss aspects of the Bill of Rights and study
                         decisions made by the U.S. Supreme Court.

Materials: Summaries of Supreme Court Cases (included in this lesson)

Advance Preparation: None

Procedure:

1. Review the Bill of Rights, it's function and contents, with students (see
    background for the teacher.)

2. Read "facts" and "issues" sections from a supreme court case found at the end
    of this lesson.

3. Allow students time to discuss the facts and issues of the case, arguing different
    points of view as appropriate.

4. After a good discussion of the legal points, have class members vote on which
    side they think should win the case.

5. Read the Supreme Court decision and reasoning.

Background for the teacher: Many of the amendments to the United States Constitution
have been challenged in court cases and interpreted by the United States Supreme
Court. These are the decisions that directly affect the interpretation of laws and the
entire court system.

                                                    © Substitute Teacher Training Institute

The Bill of Rights: **The first 10 amendments to the Constitution of the United States of America**

Amendment 1: Provides for the freedom of religion, speech, press, assembly, and petition to the government for the redress of grievances.

Amendment 2: People of the states have the right to keep weapons.

Amendment 3: People cannot be forced to house troops during peacetime, and in war this can only happen by an act of congress.

Amendment 4: Protection against unreasonable searches and seizures.

Amendment 5: An accused person cannot be forced to give evidence against himself. Due process of law guaranteed, private property cannot be taken for public use.

Amendment 6: Accused has the right to prompt public trial. There must be a fair jury and the accused has the right to a defense lawyer.

Amendment 7: Right to trial by jury in civil cases.

Amendment 8: Protection from excessive fines, and cruel and unusual punishments.

Amendment 9: The rights of the people are not limited to those stated in the constitution.

Amendment 10: Powers not given to the United States by the constitution are given to the states or the people.

Tinker v. Des Moines Independent Community School District

393 U.S. 503, 89 S. Ct. 733 (1969)

FACTS

In December of 1965, some adults and students decided to demonstrate their opposition to U.S. involvement in the Vietnam conflict by wearing black armbands during the holiday season and by fasting on December 16 and on New Year's Eve.

The principals of schools in Des Moines, Iowa heard of the plan and adopted a policy forbidding the wearing of armbands to school. Students who refused to remove such armbands would be suspended from school until they complied with the rule. Sixteen-year old John and thirteen-year-old Mary Beth Tinker, along with another student, wore the armbands to school with full knowledge of the regulation. They were suspended and did not return to school until after New Year's Day, the end of the planned period for wearing the armbands.

ISSUES

Is the wearing of a black armband as a political protest a form of speech protected by the First Amendment, and do school authorities violate students' constitutional rights by prohibiting such speech?

DECISION

Yes; a regulation prohibiting the wearing of armbands to school upon penalty of suspension is an unconstitutional denial of students' rights to free speech.

REASONING

Wearing an armband as a political protest is a symbolic act and therefore a form of "*pure speech*". The speech or expression is "*pure*" because it is not accompanied by disruptive conduct. This was a "*silent, passive expression of opinion, unaccompanied by any disorder or disturbance on the part of petitioners.*"

The regulation amounted to prohibiting a discussion of the Vietnam conflict in the hallway. Even though a few students made hostile remarks outside of class to the students wearing armbands, there were no threats or acts of violence on school premises. Without evidence that a prohibition of expression is necessary to avoid "*material and substantial interference with school work or discipline,*" it is not constitutionally permissible. Two dissenting justices would have upheld the school regulation in support of the need to maintain discipline and good order in the schools.

Distributed by the Center for Research and Development in Law-Related Education, Wake Forest University School of Law, 2714 Henning Drive, Winston-Salem NC 27106, 1-800-437-1054. The Warren E. Burger National Repository for Education Materials on Citizenship and the Constitution.

 © Substitute Teacher Training Institute

Miranda v. Arizona

(1966)

FACTS:

Ernesto Miranda was arrested at his home in Phoenix, Arizona, on suspicion of kidnapping and rape of an 18-year-old female. At the police station, a young woman identified Miranda as the offender. Miranda was taken to a room for questioning, where he confessed quickly.

Miranda was not told that he was entitled to have a lawyer present during the questioning nor that he had the right to remain silent and that anything he said could be used against him in court — at least, these rights were not stated to him clearly.

Miranda's attorney objected to the admission of the confession into evidence, but the judge overruled his objection. The jury found Miranda guilty of both kidnapping and rape, and he was sentenced to 20 to 30 years imprisonment.

Miranda claimed that he did not realize that what he told the police could be used against him at trial. When the case was appealed to the Arizona Supreme Court, the court ruled against Miranda. The court noted that Miranda's signed confession included the statement that he "*understood*" that the statement could be used against him. In addition, Miranda had not specifically requested a lawyer, so the police were not required to provide one for him.

ISSUE:

Does the constitution require that before a confession can be used in court, a suspect in police custody be informed of and understand his or her rights to an attorney and to remain silent?

DECISION:

Yes. In a 5-4 decision, the Supreme Court of the United States ruled that the confession should not have been admitted into evidence

against Miranda. The Court decided that this case, pointed out the importance of protecting individuals against overzealous police practices.

"*The mere fact that he signed a statement containing a typed-in clause that he had full knowledge of his* 'legal rights' *does not approach the knowing and intelligent waiver required to relinquish constitutional rights.*" The Court spelled out the specific warnings that police must give before questioning a person in their custody if they want to use the answers as evidence:

1. You have the right to remain silent.

2. Anything you say can and will be used against you in a court of law.

3. You have the right to talk to a lawyer and to have him present with you while you are being questioned.

4. If you cannot afford to hire a lawyer, one will be appointed to represent you before any questioning, if you wish.

5. You can decide at any time to exercise these rights and not answer any questions or make any statements.

The officer should then ask, "*Do you understand each of these rights I have explained to you?*" and "*Having these rights in mind, do you wish to talk to us now?*"

Miranda was retried and convicted without the use of the confession. This time, there was evidence that Miranda confessed his guilt to another person, and she testified against him. After serving some time, Miranda was paroled. Some years later, he was killed in a bar fight. In his pocket were the cards with the Miranda warning that he had been selling at the courthouse to support himself.

Distributed by the Center for Research and Development in Law-Related Education, Wake Forest University School of Law, 2714 Henning Drive, Winston-Salem NC 27106, 1-800-437-1054. The Warren E. Burger National Repository for Education Materials on Citizenship and the Constitution.

Terry v. Ohio

(1968)

FACTS

Police Detective McFadden was patrolling an area for shoplifters and pickpockets in downtown Cleveland — a job he held for thirty years. He became suspicious of the actions of the two men. During a short period of time, the two walked past one store a half dozen times, each time peering into the store window. Then they met briefly with a third man. Thinking the group might be "*casing*" the store before robbing it Officer McFadden followed them. They stopped again in front of the same store and talked once more with the third man.

McFadden now approached the three men. He identified himself as a police officer and asked for their names. They mumbled answers. McFadden then seized one man, who was named Terry, and used him as a shield against the others. He ordered all three into the store. McFadden then conducted what is called a "*stop-and-frisk*." That is, he stopped them and ran his hands quickly over their clothing. In the pockets of Terry and one of the others, a man called Chilton, the detective found guns. The third man was unarmed. Terry and Chilton were arrested and convicted of possessing concealed weapons.

The two defendants asked the U.S. Supreme Court to review their case. They argued that the police officer's stop-and-frisk was an unreasonable search. They claimed their right to privacy under the Fourth Amendment had been violated. The weapons had been seized without a search warrant, the men argued. And they had not been arrested at the time the guns were seized. Therefore, said Terry and Chilton, the guns should not be used as evidence against them.

The state of Ohio argued that police officers have the duty to investigate suspicious situations in order to prevent crime. And they must act reasonably to protect themselves.

ISSUE

Does the Fourth Amendment permit a reasonable search for weapons?

DECISION

Yes. The U.S. Supreme Court upheld the convictions of Terry and Chilton. Even before an arrest, said the Court, where officers reasonably believe that the person they are investigating is armed and dangerous, they have the right to conduct a limited search for weapons. Such a search is reasonable protection of the safety of the officers as well as bystanders. And it does not violate the Fourth Amendment.

Distributed by the Center for Research and Development in Law-Related Education, Wake Forest University School of Law, 2714 Henning Drive, Winston-Salem NC 27106, 1-800-437-1054. The Warren E. Burger National Repository for Education Materials on Citizenship and the Constitution.

© Substitute Teacher Training Institute

Edwards v. South Carolina

(1963)

FACTS

"*Down with segregation!*" read one protester's sign. Another read, "*You may jail our bodies but not our souls.*" Nearly 200 high school and college students were marching toward the South Carolina state house grounds in Columbia to protest discrimination against blacks.

They had set out from a nearby church in small groups. At the state house, the students were met by officials who told them they had the right to enter the grounds as long as they were peaceful. A crowd of fewer than 300 people gathered to watch the demonstration. There was no threat of violence on the part on the part of the marchers or the crowd. Police protection at all times was ample.

After a half-hour, police ordered the demonstrators to disperse within fifteen minutes or be subject to arrest. The protesters refused to leave. Instead, they sang patriotic and religious songs, stamped their feet, and clapped their hands. One of the leaders gave a speech. Fifteen minutes later they were arrested for breach of the peace. The students maintained at their trial that their freedom of expression had been denied. The state claimed that the police had acted to protect its citizens against an outbreak of violence. The case eventually was heard by the U.S. Supreme Court.

ISSUE

Does the Constitution protect peaceful demonstrations?

DECISION

Yes. The U.S. Supreme Court overturned the conviction of the demonstrators. There was no threat of violence. Police protection was ample. The capitol was an appropriate place to protest for change. A state does not have the right, said the Court, to "*make criminal the peaceful expression of unpopular views.*"

Distributed by the Center for Research and Development in Law-Related Education, Wake Forest University School of Law, 2714 Henning Drive, Winston-Salem NC 27106, 1-800-437-1054. The Warren E. Burger National Repository for Education Materials on Citizenship and the Constitution.

New Jersey v. T.L.O.

469 U.S. 325, 105 S. Ct. 733 (1985)

FACTS

A teacher at a New Jersey high school, upon discovering a 14-year-old freshman (*T.L.O.*) and her companion smoking cigarettes in a school lavatory in violation of a school rule, took them to the Principal's office, where they met with the Assistant Vice Principal. In response to the Assistant Vice Principal's questioning, T.L.O. denied that she had been smoking and claimed that she did not smoke at all. The Assistant Vice Principal demanded to see her purse. Upon opening the purse, he found a pack of cigarettes and also noticed a package of cigarette rolling papers that are commonly associated with the use of marijuana.

He then proceeded to search the purse thoroughly and found some marijuana, a pipe, plastic bags, a fairly substantial amount of money, an index card containing a list of students who owed T.L.O. money, and two letters that implicated her in marijuana dealing. Thereafter, the State brought delinquency charges against her in Juvenile Court, which, after denying her motion to suppress the evidence found in her purse, held that the Fourth Amendment applied to searches by school officials, but that the search in question was a reasonable one, and adjudged respondent to be a delinquent.

ISSUES

(1) Does the Fourth Amendment prohibition on unreasonable searches and seizures apply to searches conducted by school officials? **(2)** If so how far does that Fourth Amendment protection extend?

DECISION

Yes, the Fourth Amendment applies but the protection does not extend very far. The U.S. Supreme Court stated that the standard needed to justify such searches is reasonable suspicion, not probable cause. Reasonable suspicion was defined by the Court as reasonable suspicion that a search will reveal evidence that the student violated the law or school rules.

REASONING

Students do have a legitimate expectation of privacy. School officials are agents of the state and cannot claim immunity under the doctrine of "*in loco parentis*". Courts must apply a balancing test weighing the school officials' responsibility to maintain order and discipline in a learning environment against the students right to privacy. The Court recognized the need for flexibility in school disciplinary proceedings.

In this particular case each successive step of the search of T.L.O. lead to reasonable suspicion for the next step in the search:
- the teacher informed the official about the smoking which led to the search of the purse
- the rolling papers justified a further search into the purse
- the drug paraphernalia and the money led to the unzipping of the pockets in the purse
- the list of those owing money justified a reading of the letters.

As a result the search was reasonable.

This was a six to three decision and even the Justices who agreed with the result disagreed with their reasons for arriving at that result. In his dissenting opinion Justice Stevens stated that the contents of her purse had no bearing on the accusation made against T.LO. regarding smoking cigarettes. Mere possession of cigarettes was not even a violation of school rules therefore the search of her purse was unreasonable, he argued.

Distributed by the Center for Research and Development in Law-Related Education, Wake Forest University School of Law, 2714 Henning Drive, Winston-Salem NC 27106, 1-800-437-1054. The Warren E. Burger National Repository for Education Materials on Citizenship and the Constitution.

© Substitute Teacher Training Institute

Wisconsin v. Yoder

406 U.S. 205, 92 S. Ct. 1526 (1972)

FACTS

The Wisconsin compulsory attendance law requires that children attend public or private schools until the age of 16. Jonas Yoder, a member of the Old Order Amish religion, refused to send his daughter Frieda to school following her graduation from eighth grade. He was fined $5. There were two other parents and children who were also fined.

A basic tenet of the Amish faith is that religion pervades all life and that salvation requires living in a church community apart from worldly influence. They object to public secondary schools because the high school tends to emphasize intellectual and scientific accomplishments, self-distinction, competitiveness, worldly success, and social life with other students. Amish society emphasizes a life of "*goodness*" rather than intellect, "*wisdom*" rather than technical knowledge, and community welfare rather than competition. The conflict between worldly and nonworldly values, they argued, would do psychological harm to the Amish children.

ISSUE

Do compulsory school attendance laws, effective beyond eighth grade, violate the rights of the Amish to free exercise of their religion?

DECISION

Yes. To force the Amish to comply with the compulsory attendance law means that they must either leave the state or risk the loss of their children to a secular society.

REASONING

"*A way of life that is odd or even erratic but interferes with no rights or interests of others is not to be condemned because it is different. The Amish offer their children an ideal vocational education, instilling in them the social and political responsibilities of citizenship. There was nothing to indicate that the health, safety, or welfare of the children have been endangered by the actions of their parents.*"

Justice Douglas dissented with regard to two of the three children because they did not testify as to their own views: "*These children are* 'persons' *within the meaning of the Bill of Rights.... It is the future of the student, not the future of the parents, that is imperiled by today's decision. The child, therefore, should be given an opportunity to be heard before the State gives the exemption which we honor today.*"

Distributed by the Center for Research and Development in Law-Related Education, Wake Forest University School of Law, 2714 Henning Drive, Winston-Salem NC 27106, 1-800-437-1054. The Warren E. Burger National Repository for Education Materials on Citizenship and the Constitution.

A Citizenship Test

What does it take for a person from a foreign land to become an American citizen? In addition to being a person of good moral character, they must be at least 18 years old, have a solid grasp of the English language, and pass a citizenship test. Each year about one million immigrants take this test. They know their American history. Do you?

Below are 30 questions taken from the Immigration and Naturalization Service (INS) citizenship question pool. Write down the answer, or your best guess, then check your answers. You need to answer at least 18 of the 30 questions correctly to pass.

1. How many stars are there on our flag?

2. What do the stars on the flag mean?

3. What color are the stripes?

4. What do the stripes on the flag mean?

5. What is the date of Independence Day?

6. Independence from whom?

7. What do we call a change to the Constitution?

8. How many branches are there in our government?

9. How many full terms can a president serve?

10. Who nominates judges of the Supreme Court?

11. How many Supreme Court justices are there?

12. Who was the main writer of the Declaration of Independence?

13. What holiday was celebrated for the first time by American colonists?

14. Who wrote the Star-Spangled Banner?

15. What is the minimum voting age in the United States?

16. Who was president during the Civil War?

17. Which president is called the "Father of our Country?"

18. What is the 50th state of the Union?

19. What is the name of the ship that brought the Pilgrims to America?

20. Who has the power to declare war?

21. What were the 13 original states of the United States called?

22. In what year was the Constitution written?

23. What is the introduction to the Constitution called?

24. Which president was the first Commander in Chief of the United States Army and Navy?

25. In what month do we vote for the president?

26. How many times may a senator be re-elected?

27. Who signs bills into law?

28. Who elects the president of the United States?

29. How many states are there in the United States?

30. Who becomes president if both the president and vice president die?

© Substitute Teacher Training Institute

Answers

Citizenship Test ANSWER KEY

1. 50

2. One for each state in the Union.

3. Red and White

4. They represent the 13 original states.

5. July 4th

6. England

7. amendments

8. Three

9. Two

10. The President

11. Nine

12. Thomas Jefferson

13. Thanksgiving

14. Francis Scott Key

15. 18

16. Abraham Lincoln

17. George Washington

18. Hawaii

19. The Mayflower

20. The Congress

21. Colonies

22. 1787

23. The Preamble

24. George Washington

25. November

26. There is no limit at the present time.

27. The President

28. The Electoral College

29. 50

30. Speaker of the House of Representatives

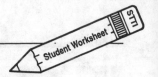

The Political Parties

There are two main political parties in United States government, the Democrats and the Republicans. After reading the brief overview of each party, write about the elements of each party that you either agree or disagree with and summarize by indicating the party you feel best represents your political views.

THE DEMOCRATIC PARTY

The democratic party has had a reputation for being liberal, for appealing to low-income groups, for expanding civil rights protection, and for believing that government is a legitimate vehicle for solving social problems.

THE REPUBLICAN PARTY

The republican party is often considered the conservative party. In the past, republicans have supported increased spending on defense and decreased spending on domestic, education, and welfare programs. In general republicans seek a reduction in the size of government by decreasing the government regulation and increasing the privatization of many government programs.

In the space below, briefly summarize your own political views and how they correspond with those of the political parties above. Indicate which political party you feel most closely affiliated with and why.

_____
_____
_____
_____
_____
_____
_____
_____
_____
_____
_____
_____
_____
_____
_____
_____
_____
_____

© Substitute Teacher Training Institute

Landmark Decisions

The Supreme Court, often referred to as the highest court in the land, is the final authority in the United States law system. It is made up of nine justices, one of whom serves as chief justice. The responsibilities of the Supreme Court include hearing cases between states, cases involving other countries, and cases where a federal law has been broken. The Supreme Court also has the duty to review acts of Congress and the President to determine if they are unconstitutional. Additionally, each year the Supreme Court is asked to hear thousands of cases on appeal from a lower court. Throughout history, the Supreme Court has made many decisions which have shaped our society. Review the "Landmark Decisions" below and then select one ruling and briefly write how you think society would be different today if the Supreme Court had made the opposite decision.

- **1803**   **Marbury vs. Madison.** Chief Justice Marshall asserted the Court's right to a judicial review — to overturn a law as unconstitutional.

- **1932**   **Powell vs. Alabama.** A person on trial for a capital crime is entitled to legal counsel even if the state must provide it. This ruling was later broadened to include the right to legal counsel for any person on trial for a crime that could involve a jail term.

- **1954**   **Brown vs. Board of Education.** Separate but equal schools for blacks and whites are ruled unconstitutional.

- **1962**   **Engel vs. Vitale.** Public schools cannot constitutionally require students to recite prayers.

- **1973**   **Roe vs. Wade.** State laws prohibiting abortion during a woman's first six months of pregnancy are ruled unconstitutional.

_____
_____
_____
_____
_____
_____
_____
_____
_____
_____
_____
_____
_____
_____
_____
_____
_____
_____
_____
_____
_____

The Constitution

Ratified in 1788 the constitution of the United States has served as the basis for U.S. government ever since. It set up a federal government system with three branches, legislative, executive, and judicial, while allowing states to retain many rights and responsibilities. Try to correctly fill in the blanks to complete the preamble to this historical document.

Preamble

We the _____ of the United States, in order to _____ a more perfect _____, establish _____, insure domestic _____, provide for the common _____, promote the general _____, and secure the blessings of _____ to ourselves and our _____, do ordain and _____ this _____ for the _____ States of _____.

Throughout the 200+ years the constitution has been in place, relatively few amendments have been added to the original document. However, the amendments to the constitution, and rights guaranteed by them, are perhaps the most critical documentation of citizen rights in our society today. Can you match the amendment number and date to the responsibility, right, or law it secures.

_____ Amendment 1 (1791)   A.   Voting rights for blacks.

_____ Amendment 2 (1791)   B.   Lowered the voting age to eighteen.

_____ Amendment 4 (1791)   C.   Prohibition of alcohol.

_____ Amendment 5 (1791)   D.   Limited presidential terms of office.

____ Amendment 13 (1865)   E.   Presidential succession outlined.

____ Amendment 15 (1870)   F.   Do not have to testify against oneself.

____ Amendment 18 (1919)   G.   Freedom of religion, speech, press, assembly, and petition.

____ Amendment 19 (1920)   H.   Right to bear arms.

____ Amendment 21 (1933)   I.   Warrants needed for searches and seizures.

____ Amendment 22 (1951)   J.   Voting rights for women.

____ Amendment 25 (1967)   K.   The repeal of the prohibition amendment.

____ Amendment 26 (1971)   L.   The abolition of slavery.

© Substitute Teacher Training Institute

The Constitution ANSWER KEY

Preamble

We the people of the United State, in order to form a more perfect union, establish justice, insure domestic tranquillity, provide for the common defense, promote the general welfare, and secure the blessings of liberty to ourselves and our posterity, do ordain and establish this Constitution for the United States of America.

Constitutional Amendments

Amendment 1 (1791)	G.	Freedom of religion, speech, press, assembly, and petition.
Amendment 2 (1791)	H.	Right to bear arms.
Amendment 4 (1791)	I.	Warrants needed for searches and seizures.
Amendment 5 (1791)	F.	Do not have to testify against oneself.
Amendment 13 (1865)	L.	The abolition of slavery.
Amendment 15 (1870)	A.	Voting rights for blacks.
Amendment 18 (1919)	C.	Prohibition of alcohol.
Amendment 19 (1920)	J.	Voting rights for women.
Amendment 21 (1933)	K.	The repeal of the prohibition amendment.
Amendment 22 (1951)	D.	Limited presidential terms of office.
Amendment 25 (1967)	E.	Presidential succession outlined.
Amendment 26 (1971)	B.	Lowered the voting age to eighteen.

NAME _____

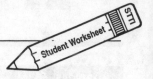

Presidential Trivia

Matching

_____ 1. George Washington   A. Made the decision to use the atomic bomb against Japan.

_____ 2. John Tyler   B. The only president to serve two terms which did not follow each other.

_____ 3. Grover Cleveland   C. Became the first president to hold regular press conferences to explain his policies.

_____ 4. Harry S. Truman   D. As president, he created over more than one million acres of national forests and parks.

_____ 5. Gerald R. Ford   E. Became the first vice-president to take over after a president had died in office.

_____ 6. Woodrow Wilson   F. Left school around the age of 14 to become a surveyor.

_____ 7. Theodore Roosevelt   G. The only man to be both president and vice-president without being elected to either office.

True or False

_____ 1. President Lyndon B. Johnson was sworn into office aboard the presidential airplane.

_____ 2. President James Madison is referred to as "the father of the Declaration of Independence."

_____ 3. President John Quincy Adams was a poor public speaker with only an elementary knowledge of English.

_____ 4. President William H. Taft began the tradition of throwing out the first baseball of the major league baseball season.

_____ 5. Prior to becoming president, George Bush served as director of the Central Intelligence Agency.

_____ 6. President James Garfield amazed people by writing Latin with one hand and Greek with the other, at the same time.

_____ 7. President Andrew Johnson spent his childhood evenings reading books by the fire.

Which Does Not Belong

1. James Monroe   A. Monroe Doctrine   B. Louisiana Purchase   C. Civil War Soldier

2. Abraham Lincoln   A. Cherry Tree   B. Emancipation Proclamation   C. Assassination

3. Ronald Reagan   A. Movie Star   B. Barbara   C. I don't remember.

4. John F. Kennedy   A. Oldest President   B. Bay of Pigs   C. Lee Harvey Oswald

5. Dwight D. Eisenhower   A. I like Ike   B. Career Soldier   C. Wheelchair

6. Bill Clinton   A. NAFTA   B. White House dogs   C. Arkansas

© Substitute Teacher Training Institute

Presidential Trivia ANSWER KEY

Matching

1. George Washington   F.   Left school around the age of 14 to become a surveyor.

2. John Tyler   E.   Became the first vice-president to take over after a president had died in office.

3. Grover Cleveland   B.   The only president to serve two terms which did not follow each other.

4. Harry S. Truman   A.   Made the decision to use the atomic bomb against Japan.

5. Gerald R. Ford   G.   The only man to be both president and vice-president without being elected to either office.

6. Woodrow Wilson   C.   Became the first president to hold regular press conferences to explain his policies.

7. Theodore Roosevelt   D.   As president, he created over more than one million acres of national forests and parks.

True or False

T   1.   President Lyndon B. Johnson was sworn into office aboard the presidential airplane.

F   2.   President James Madison is referred to as "the father of the Declaration of Independence." (He is considered the father of the Constitution.)

F   3.   President John Quincy Adams was a poor public speaker with only an elementary knowledge of English. (He spoke seven languages before he attended Harvard and was nicknamed "Old Man Eloquent")

T   4.   President William H. Taft began the tradition of throwing out the first baseball of the major league baseball season.

T   5.   Prior to becoming president, George Bush served as director of the Central Intelligence Agency.

T   6.   President James Garfield amazed people by writing Latin with one hand and Greek with the other, at the same time.

F.   7.   President Andrew Johnson spent his childhood evenings reading books by the fire. (He did not learn to read and write until he was married and taught by his wife.)

Which Does Not Belong ANSWER KEY

1. James Monroe

   A. Monroe Doctrine   B. Louisiana Purchase   C. Civil War Soldier(X)

2. Abraham Lincoln

   A. Cherry Tree (X)   B. Emancipation   C. Assassination
                            Proclamation

3. Ronald Reagan

   A. Movie Star   B. Barbara (X)   C. I don't remember

4. John F. Kennedy

   A. Oldest President (X)   B. Bay of Pigs   C. Lee Harvey Oswald

5. Dwight D. Eisenhower

   A. I like Ike   B. Career Soldier   C. Wheelchair(X)

6. Bill Clinton

   A. NAFTA   B. White House dogs(X)   C. Arkansas

© Substitute Teacher Training Institute

This Year in History

Time: 30 minutes

Objective: Students will attempt to identify the things for which the current year will be remembered.

Materials: paper and pencils

Optional Materials: news magazines, news papers, etc.

Advance Preparation: none

Procedure:

1.   Divide the class into small groups.

2.   List categories in which to identify specific events or fads of the year, such as the ones listed below.

A.	World Events	G.	Movies
B.	National Events	H.	Clothing Styles
C.	Political Events	I.	Shoes
D.	Music	J.	Toys
E.	Commercials	K.	Candy Bars
F.	TV Shows	L.	Inventions

3.   Have students brainstorm as many items as they can for each category.

4.   As a class, compile a master list with one or two items in each category which best represents the time period.

5.   Discuss how students think the events and fads of this year will change or affect society in the years to come.

20 Events

Listed below are 20 events that changed American History. Match them with their description on the right.

_____ 1. Plymouth Colony

_____ 2. Slavery

_____ 3. Declaration of Independence

_____ 4. Ratification of the Constitution

_____ 5. 1800 Election

_____ 6. Louisiana Purchase

_____ 7. Seneca Falls Convention

_____ 8. Secession

_____ 9. Emancipation Proclamation

_____ 10. Transcontinental Railroad

_____ 11. Pullman Strike

_____ 12. Spanish-American War

_____ 13. Treaty of Versailles

_____ 14. National Origins Act, 1924

_____ 15. The Great Depression

_____ 16. Attack on Pearl Harbor

_____ 17. Montgomery Bus Boycott

_____ 18. Cuban Missile Crisis

_____ 19. Vietnam War

_____ 20. The Reagan Election

A. This protest set the civil rights movement in motion.

B. Marked the United States' arrival as a major world power.

C. Launched the movement that would help women win full citizenship, including the right to vote.

D. The establishment of a blueprint for American government.

E. Colonists began importing Africans to meet a severe labor shortage.

F. This legislation closed America's open door to immigrants.

G. A long bloody war that divided America and helped create a generation that mistrusted the government.

H. Presidential decree abolishing slavery.

I. The first major confrontation between the federal government and the labor movement.

J. Pilgrim settlers established a new settlement in North America.

K. Doubled the size of the United States and accelerated territorial expansion.

L. A confrontation with the Soviet Union that threatened to turn the Cold War into a nuclear war.

M. Economic crisis which left millions of Americans without jobs, homes, or food.

N. A decisive election in which the American people rejected big government and the welfare state.

O. The creation of a nation by the South and beginning of a long and terrible war.

P. Proclamation of the independence of a new nation which would be ruled by the people rather than a king.

Q. Marked the official beginning of the two party system with a peaceful, and orderly transfer of power.

R. A surprise Japanese attack that brought the United States into a second world war.

S. Ended the First World War and set the conditions that led to the Second.

T. Transformed the social and economic life of America by linking the regions of the nation.

Select one of the events from the above list. Turn this paper over and write about how American life would be different today if this event had not occurred, or write a brief summary elaborating on the details of the event. You may want to use your textbook as a reference.

© Substitute Teacher Training Institute

Answers

20 Events ANSWER KEY

1. Plymouth Colony   J. Pilgrim settlers established a new settlement in North America.

2. Slavery   E. Colonists began importing Africans to meet a severe labor shortage.

3. Declaration of Independence   P. Proclamation of the independence of a new nation which would be ruled by the people rather than a king.

4. Ratification of the Constitution   D. The establishment of a blueprint for American government.

5. 1800 Election   Q. Marked the official beginning of the two party system with a peaceful, and orderly transfer of power.

6. Louisiana Purchase   K. Doubled the size of the United States and accelerated territorial expansion.

7. Seneca Falls Convention   C. Launched the movement that would help women win full citizenship, including the right to vote.

8. Secession   O. The creation of a nation by the South and beginning of a long and terrible war.

9. Emancipation Proclamation   H. Presidential decree abolishing slavery.

10. Transcontinental Railroad   T. Transformed the social and economic life of America by linking the regions of the nation.

11. Pullman Strike   I. The first major confrontation between the federal government and the labor movement.

12. Spanish-American War   B. Marked the United States' arrival as a major world power.

13. Treaty of Versailles   S. Ended the First World War and set the conditions that led to the Second.

14. National Origins Act, 1924   F. This legislation closed America's open door to immigrants.

15. The Great Depression   M. Economic crisis which left millions of Americans without jobs, homes, or food.

16. Attack on Pearl Harbor   T. A surprise Japanese attack that brought the United States into a second world war.

17. Montgomery Bus Boycott   A. This protest set the civil rights movement in motion.

18. Cuban Missile Crisis   L. A confrontation with the Soviet Union that threatened to turn the Cold War into a nuclear war.

19. Vietnam War   G. A long bloody war that divided America and helped create a generation that mistrusted the government.

20. The Reagan Election   N. A decisive election in which the American people rejected big government and the welfare state.

Historic Timeline

Arrange the historical events below in the order that you think they occurred. Then check your answers to see how accurate your historical timeline is.

Group 1 (2600 BC - 1547)

Chinese Develop Paper   1. _____

Magna Charta   2. _____

The Great Wall of China   3. _____

Ivan the Terrible rules as the first Russian Czar   4. _____

First Use of Gunpowder   5. _____

Fall of Rome   6. _____

Pyramids of Giza   7. _____

Canterbury Tales Written   8. _____

First Olympic Games   9. _____

Copernicus Revolutionizes Astronomy   10. _____

Group 2 (1592 - 1905)

Civil War in the United States   11. _____

Einstein's Theory of Relativity   12. _____

Telephone Invented   13. _____

Benjamin Franklin's Kite   14. _____

Ford develops mass production   15. _____

Shakespeare begins his career as a playwright 16. _____

Darwin publishes, *Origin of the Species*   17. _____

Newton's Laws of Gravity and Motion   18. _____

The American Revolution   19. _____

Pilgrims land at Plymouth Rock   20. _____

Group 3 (1919 - 1995)

Resignation of President Nixon   21. _____

Iran Hostage Crisis   22. _____

Desert Storm   23. _____

Sputnik and the Space Race   24. _____

Oklahoma City Bombing   25. _____

Penicillin Discovered   26. _____

Berlin Wall Erected   27. _____

Tiananmen Square Demonstration   28. _____

Treaty of Versailles   29. _____

United Nations Established   30. _____

© Substitute Teacher Training Institute

Answers

Historic Timeline Answer Key

1.	2600 BC	Pyramids of Giza
2.	776 BC	First Olympic Games
3.	214 BC	The Great Wall of China
4.	100 AD	Chinese Develop Paper
5.	476 AD	Fall of Rome
6.	950 AD	First Use of Gunpowder
7.	1215	Magna Charta
8.	1387	Canterbury Tales Written
9.	1530	Copernicus Revolutionizes Astronomy
10.	1547	Ivan the Terrible rules as the first Russian Czar
11.	1592	Shakespeare begins his career as a playwright
12.	1620	Pilgrims land at Plymouth Rock
13.	1664	Newton's Laws of Gravity and Motion
14.	1752	Benjamin Franklin's Kite
15.	1775-1783	The American Revolution
16.	1859	Darwin publishes, *Origin of the Species*
17.	1861-1865	Civil War in the United States
18.	1876	Telephone Invented
19.	1903	Ford develops mass production
20.	1905	Einstein's Theory of Relativity
21	1919	Treaty of Versailles
22.	1928	Penicillin Discovered
23.	1945	United Nations Established
24.	1957	Sputnik and the Space Race
25.	1961	Berlin Wall Erected
26.	1974	Resignation of President Nixon
27.	1979-1981	Iran Hostage Crisis
28.	1989	Tiananmen Square Demonstration
29.	1991	Desert Storm
30.	1995	Oklahoma City Bombing

If History Were Altered

1. How would the world be different today if, the colonists had not won the Revolutionary War and the new country had remained under British rule?

   _____
   _____
   _____
   _____

2. How would the world be different today if, electricity had never been invented?

   _____
   _____
   _____
   _____

3. How would the world be different today if, the atomic bomb had not been used against the Japanese in World War II?

   _____
   _____
   _____
   _____

4. How would the world be different today if, Columbus and his ships had perished at sea and never reached the American Continents?

   _____
   _____
   _____
   _____

5. How would the world be different today if, travel by airplane had never been developed?

   _____
   _____
   _____
   _____

© Substitute Teacher Training Institute

Leaving a Legacy

A legacy is anything handed down from one generation to the next. Suppose you wanted to leave a legacy for those who will come after you, filled with information and insights about the world and time in which you now live. Would you organize the information in a book, a video, as objects in a box, a scrapbook filled with pictures, a hand-made quilt, a painting or work of art? What type of information would you want to preserve, historical facts, cultural fads, family history, or perhaps personal thoughts and feelings?

On the lines below share how you would prepare your legacy and the information you would want to convey down through the years.

_____
_____
_____
_____
_____
_____
_____
_____
_____
_____
_____
_____
_____
_____
_____
_____
_____
_____
_____
_____
_____
_____
_____
_____
_____
_____
_____
_____
_____
_____
_____
_____
_____
_____
_____
_____
_____
_____

Point of View

Time: 30 minutes

Objective: Students will practice writing from different points of view.

Materials: pencil and paper

Advance Preparation: List points of view on the board.

Procedure:

1.   Hold up a common object in the classroom (ruler, tape dispenser, key, tablet, stapler, etc.).

2.   Discuss what the object is and what it is used for.

3.   Ask the students to choose a point of view from the board, then write a brief paragraph from the selected point of view.

4.   Instruct students not to tell anyone the point of view they have chosen.

5.   Have volunteers read their paragraph aloud and then allow class members to guess which point of view the reader selected.
      Example Points of View:
      •   Tell a story about the object to a kindergarten class.
      •   A journal entry of an archeologist who dug up this object two hundred years from now.
      •   You are from another planet and you are writing home to explain how the object is used on earth.
      •   Write a memo to the principal explaining why this object should be purchased for every student in the school.
      •   Explain to someone who has never seen this object how it is used.
      •   Write specific details about the object so that it could be distinguished from similar objects.

6.   Have students select another object in the classroom and write about it without mentioning it by name.

7.   Trade papers among class members and have them try to identify the object the student has written about.

                                              © Substitute Teacher Training Institute

Writing & Revising

Time: 5-45 minutes

Objective: Students will practice their writing and editing skills.

Materials: pencil and paper

Advance Preparation: Select a writing prompt for the students. Create a handout, write it on the board or be prepared to give it verbally.

This activity can fill five minutes or an entire class hour depending on the complexity of the writing prompt, and at which step students stop work to turn in their paper for teacher evaluation.

Procedure:

1.   Provide the class with a writing prompt and time limit for completing the first draft of their work.

2.   Have students exchange papers and edit one another's work for content and technical components.

3.   Allow students time to discuss their editorial comments with one another, getting a second opinion from other students, if time permits.

4.   After the editing process, have students complete a second draft of their work and hand it in for teacher evaluation.

Writing Prompts:

A.   Write an invitation to a social event, real or imaginary, formal or casual.

B.   Write a letter to a national news agency convincing them to cover a recent, or upcoming event at your school.

C.   Write a letter to the school principal about changing an existing school rule or policy. Explain how and why it should be changed.

D.   Write a menu for a new restaurant in town.

E.   Write a chronological report of everything you have done so far today.

Writing Prompts: (Continued)

F. Write an outline of your life. Include events you anticipate will happen in the future.

G. Write a letter to a music company explaining a billing mistake they made on your last order from their company.

H. Write a brief essay about what life as a street light would be like.

I. Write a description of eating ice cream.

J. Write an evaluation of the pen or pencil you are using.

K. Write a memo to your boss asking him for a raise.

L. Write a grocery shopping list for Thanksgiving dinner.

M. Write a synopsis of a book you have recently read.

N. Write a newspaper article about current fashion trends or a recent sporting event.

O. Write a recipe for a new dessert you have created.

Spot 20

Lulu is away at camp. She wrote the following letter to her best friend, after curfew, by the light of a flashlight, under the covers last night. Usually a very good writer, she made a few typographical errors (20 to be exact) in her letter. Can you spot and circle all twenty errors?

July 12, 1697

Dear Emily;

Greatings from camp! You would not believe the awful time I am having. The first day my bags were run over by the bus as it pulled out of the parking lot. All of the chips I had packed for late night snacks were crushed to dust and deposited throughout my clothes. It was an omen of badd things to come.

That night it rained, and wouldn't you know it, my cot was positioned directly below a leak in the cabin roof? Need less to say I woke up soggy and I've been sneezing ever since. By the time I hanged up my wet blankets and made it to breakfast the only foold left was cold pancakes and orange juice with unidentified floating objects in it. Ugh!

The first morning we spent most of the time at the lake. Other than the fact that the water was icey cold, our canoe capsized, and my glases are now quietly resting somewhere at the bottom of Lake Wet, it was tons of fun. That afternoon I went on a nature hike. I can now identify two kinds of pinetrees, a three varieties of wild flowers, an edible berry, and Poison Oak. The Poison Oak I studied up close and personal, which left me trying not to scratch for the rest of of the evening.

The secon night passed without incident, unless you want to count the family of mice that spent the dark hours traversing the cabin floor to raid the cookies someone had left out. They were actully kindof cute.

Today it rained, so we had to spend the entire day in the lodge. In the morning I tried to make a bird house out of craft sticks. It turned out looking more like a condemmed building than anything a bird would ever want to live in. I spent the afternoon learning how to weave a basket. It was looking great until the person next to me accidentally sat on it. After dinner we learned camp songs. you know, the kind that once you get in your head you can't get rid of. So now I'm breaking curfew, to write to you from under my covers, to the tune of Row Row Row You Boat.

Just two more weeks and this joyous adventure will be over. I'll give you a call when I get home, if I survive that long

See you soon,

Lulu

SPOT 20 ANSWER KEY — Corrections in BOLD

July 12, **1997**

Dear Emily(**,**)*

Greetings from camp! You would not believe the awful time I am having. The first day my bags were run over by the bus as it pulled out of the parking lot. All of the chips I had packed for late night snacks were crushed to dust and deposited throughout my clothes. It was an omen of **bad** things to come.

That night it rained, and wouldn't you know it, my cot was positioned directly below a leak in the cabin roof. **Needless** to say I woke up soggy and I've been sneezing ever since. By the time I **hung** up my wet blankets and made it to breakfast the only **food** left was cold pancakes and orange juice with unidentified floating objects in it. Ugh!

The first morning we spent most of the time at the lake. Other than the fact that the water was **icy** cold, our canoe capsized, and my **glasses** are now quietly resting somewhere at the **bottom** of Lake Wet, it was tons of fun. That afternoon I went on a nature hike. I can now identify two kinds of **pine trees**, (**delete a**) three varieties of wild flowers, an edible berry, and Poison Oak. The Poison Oak I studied up close and personal, which left me trying not to scratch for the rest of (**delete second of**) the evening.

The **second** night passed without incident, unless you want to count the family of mice that spent the dark hours traversing the cabin floor to raid the cookies someone had left out. They were **actually kind of** cute.

Today it rained, so we had to spend the entire day in the lodge. In the morning I tried to make a bird house out of craft sticks. It turned out looking more like a **condemned** building than anything a bird would ever want to live in. I spent the afternoon learning how to weave a basket. It was looking great until the person next to me accidentally sat on it. After dinner we learned camp songs. you know, the kind that once you get in your head you can't get rid of. So now I'm breaking curfew, to write to you from under my covers, to the tune of (**"**)Row Row Row **Your** Boat.(**"**)

Just two more weeks and this joyous adventure will be over. I'll give you a call when I get home, if I survive that long(**.**)

See you soon,

Lulu

The Cow Jumped Over The Refrigerator?

Written below are three very familiar nursery rhymes with strategic words missing. Fill in the blanks
and then in the margin draw an illustration depicting your version of an old favorite.

Humpty Dumpty

Humpty Dumpty sat on a _____.

Humpty Dumpty had a great _____.

All the kings horses, and all the king's _____,

Couldn't _____.

Jack and Jill

Jack and Jill went _____,

To fetch _____ ;

Jack _____ ,

And Jill _____.

Mary Had a _____

Mary had a _____,

Its _____ was _____ as snow;

And everywhere that _____

The _____ was sure to _____.

Pieces of a Puzzle

In many ways a story is like a puzzle. A story can be broken down into individual pieces such as good guys, bad guys, supporting characters, settings, beginning, ending, conflict, etc. Until all of the pieces are arranged correctly they may not make a lot of sense, but skillfully pieced together to form a complete picture, they can tell a powerful story. Choose one story piece from each column in the chart below and then put them together to create an original story of your own.

Protagonist (Good Guy)	Antagonist (Bad Guy)	Supporting Character	Setting	Conflict	Conclusion
chef	dentist	doctor	New York City	man vs. self	tragedy
nurse	father	best friend	beach	man vs. nature	to be continued
lawyer	college student	dog	foreign country	man vs. society	happy
teacher	athlete	waitress	hotel	good vs. evil	bad guy wins
cowboy	politician	movie star	ranch	something stolen	everyone dies
computer expert	thief	artist	cemetery	young vs. old	guy gets girl
detective	jockey	zoo keeper	used car lot	man vs. machine	only a dream
author	sister	computer	school	a dying request	the butler did it

NAME

© Substitute Teacher Training Institute

A Dozen Puzzlers

1. A lady goes to the well with two jugs. One holds exactly nine quarts and the other holds exactly five quarts. She needs exactly three quarts of water for her soup. Using only two jugs, which she cannot mark in any way, how can she get the three quarts?

Answer She fills the nine-quart jug and pours five quarts from it into the five-quart jug. She empties the five-quart jug and pours the remaining four-quarts left in the nine-quart jug into the five-quart jug. Now she fills the nine-quart jug again and pours one quart in to fill up the five-quart jug. Then she empties the five-quart jug and fills it again with five quarts from the eight quarts that are in the nine-quart jug. And now, she has three quarts left in the nine-quart jug—just enough to make her soup!

2. Five hundred people shopped in a candy store and spent a total of $500. The women each spent $1, the children spent one cent each, and the men each spent $5. How many men shopped in the store? How many women? How many children?

Answer Four hundred children, one woman, ninety-nine men.

3. The zoo just bought exactly one ton of animals (2000 pounds): a zebra, a wolf, a Lynx, a peacock, and a buffalo. The zebra makes up forty-five percent of the total weight, and the wolf weighs nine times the combined weight of the Lynx and the peacock. The average weight of the Lynx and the peacock is five-tenths percent of the weight of the zebra. How much does the buffalo weigh?

Answer 1,010 pounds.

4.   Millie, the marble packer, arranged all her marbles in one solid square and found that she had two hundred marbles left over. She then received a new shipment of one thousand marbles. She increased two sides of her original square by five marbles and found she was twenty-five marbles short of completing the second square. How many marbles did Millie have to start with?

Answer   14,600 marbles.

5.   If you had just bought the real estate pictured below and wanted to subdivide it into eight lots, each of the exact same size and shape, how would you do it?

Answer

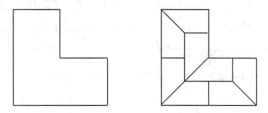

6.   Draw a square and divide it into nine smaller squares by drawing two vertical and two horizontal lines. Using each number only once, arrange the numbers one through nine in the squares so that they total fifteen across, down, and diagonally.

Answer

2	9	4
7	5	3
6	1	8

7.   Without leaving any digit out or repeating a digit, arrange the numbers one through seven so that when added together, they equal one hundred.

Answer   15 + 36 + 47 + 2 = 100

                                          © Substitute Teacher Training Institute

8. Write down any number. Multiply by two. Add eighteen. Divide by two. Subtract your original number. No matter what you started with, your answer is nine!

Answer

43	x	2	=	86
86	+	18	=	104
104	÷	2	=	52
52	-	43	=	9

9. Write down any three-digit number. Reverse the number—if you had one hundred twenty-three, write three hundred twenty-one— and subtract the smaller from the larger. Write down the answer. Now reverse the answer and add. Your answer is one thousand eighty-nine, no matter what number you started with!

Answer 873
-378
495
+594
1089

10. If you will tell me which column or columns the age of your car is in, I will tell you how old it is.

A	B	C	D
1	2	4	8
3	3	5	9
5	6	6	10
7	7	7	11
9	10	12	12
11	11	13	13
13	14	14	14
15	15	15	15

Answer Add the top number of the columns you find the age in. The total will give you the age.

11. The oldest mathematical puzzle in the world is said to be this four thousand year-old puzzler translated from the Ahmes Papyrus:

There is a number such that if the whole of it is added to one-seventh of it, the result will make nineteen.

Can you figure it out?

Answer

$$x + x/7 = 19$$

$$7(x + x/7) = 19 \times 7$$

$$8x = 133$$

$$x = 16\ 5/8$$

12. There are over forty patterns of four squares that add up to thirty-four in Durer's Magic Square. How many can you find?

16	3	2	13
5	10	11	8
9	6	7	12
4	15	14	1

Answer A few of them are: all rows, all columns, the two diagonals, four corner squares, four center squares. Carry on!

© Substitute Teacher Training Institute

Number Phrases

How quickly can you decipher the number phrases below? The first one has been completed for you.

A.   26 - L. of the A.   **Answer:** 26 letters of the alphabet

B.   7 - W. of the W.

C.   54 - C. in a D. (with the J.)

D.   88 - P. K.

E.   18 - H. on a G. C.

F.   90 - D. in a R. A.

G.   4 - Q. in a G.

H.   24 - H. in a D.

I.   11 - P. on a F. T.

J.   29 - D. in F. in a L. Y.

K.   76 - T. L. the B. P.

L.   20,000 - L. U. T. S.

M.   7 - D. of the W.

N.   12 E. in a D.

O.   3 - B. M. (S. H. T. R.!)

Number Phrases ANSWER KEY

A.   26 letters of the alphabet

B.   7 wonders of the world

C.   54 cards in a deck (with the Joker)

D.   88 piano keys

E.   18 holes on a golf course

F.   90 degrees in a right angle

G.   4 quarts in a gallon

H.   24 hours in a day

I.   11 players on a football team

J.   29 days in February in a Leap Year

K.   76 trombones lead the big parade

L.   20,000 leagues under the sea

M.   7 days of the week

N.   12 eggs in a dozen

O.   3 blind mice (see how they run!)

If you don't have time to photocopy the worksheet, copy one or more of the number phrases on the board. Then challenge the students to guess the phrase.

© Substitute Teacher Training Institute

NAME _____

Interesting Water Facts

Did you know that growing the food for one person, for one day requires about 1,700 gallons of water? Just think how many gallons are needed to grow the food for all of the students at your school. In completing this worksheet you will compute and learn many interesting facts about water

FACT: Americans use an average of 130 gallons of water, per person, per day.

1. How many gallons would a family of five use in one day? _____

2. How many gallons are used by the people in your household? _____

3. How many gallons will be used by the people in this class today? _____

4. How many gallons would one person use over in a year's time? _____

5. Approximately how many gallons have you used in your lifetime? _____

FACT: Water is a bargain.

The average cost for a gallon of water is less than one cent per gallon. The average cost for a gallon of milk is $2.34. Complete the chart below to illustrate how much more daily activities would cost if the price of water was similar to that of milk.

Daily Activity	Water Used	Current Cost	Cost at $2.34 /gal	Difference Between Costs
6. washing a car	100 gallons	< $1.00		
7. doing a load of laundry	47 gallons	< 47 ¢		
8. running the dishwasher	60 gallons	< 60 ¢		
9. brushing your teeth	3 gallons	< 3 ¢		
10. a 10 minute shower	55 gallons	< 55 ¢		

FACT: It takes a lot of water to produce things we use and consume everyday.

Match the amount of water needed for production for each item below.

11. water needed to grow one ear of corn   136 gallons
12. water a cow needs to drink to produce a gallon of milk   1,400 gallons
13. water used to produce a family car   3 gallons
14. water used to produce a loaf of bread   26 gallons
15. water used to prepare a hamburger, fries, and drink   100,000 gallons

Fact: Every drip counts!

16. If a dripping faucet drips a cup of water every hour, how many gallons of water will "drip" down the drain every year? (HINT: THERE ARE 16 CUPS IN A GALLON) _____

17. Many houses in America have toilets that leak. A leaking toilet can waste as much as 60 gallons of water everyday. Suppose that one-third of the students in your class had one leaky toilet in their home. How much water would be wasted in the homes of your classmates every year? _____

18. Turning off the water while brushing your teeth can save as much as two gallons of water every time you brush. If you turn off the faucet as you brush your teeth two times each day, how much water would be saved over the course of one year? _____

Interesting Water Facts ANSWER KEY

1. 650 gallons

2. no. in household x 130

3. no. in class x 130

4. 47,450 gallons

5. 130 x 365 x age in years

6. $234.00; $233.00

7. $109.98; $109.51

8. $140.40; $139.80

9. $7.02; $6.99

10. $128.70; $128.15

11. 26 gallons

12. 3 gallons

13. 100,000 gallons

14. 136 gallons

15. 1,400 gallons

16. 547.5 gallons

17. no. in class ÷ 3 x 60 x 365

18. 1,460 gallons

© Substitute Teacher Training Institute

Number Patterns

Find the next three numbers in the sequences below.

1. 150, 200, 250, 300, _____ , _____ , _____

2. 1, 7, 49, 343, _____ , _____ , _____

3. 654, 641, 628, 615, _____ , _____ , _____

4. 13312, 3328, 832, 208, _____ , _____ , _____

5. 72, 78, 84, 90, _____ , _____ , _____

6. 23, 27.5, 32, 36.5, _____ , _____ , _____

7. 123, 234, 345, 456, _____ , _____ , _____

8. 115, 105, 96, 88, _____ , _____ , _____

9. 86, 84, 80, 74, _____ , _____ , _____

10. 2, 3, 4.5, 6.75, _____ , _____ , _____

11. 99, 98, 96, 93, _____ , _____ , _____

12. 11, 43, 75, 107, _____ , _____ , _____

13. 2, 5, 11, 20, _____ , _____ , _____

14. 842, 759, 676, 593, _____ , _____ , _____

15. 1, 2, 4, 7, _____ , _____ , _____

16. 5, 16, 38, 82, _____ , _____ , _____

17. 12, 18, 27, 40.5, _____ , _____ , _____

18. 2, 3, 5, 8, 13, _____ , _____ , _____

19. 4, 13, 40, 121, _____ , _____ , _____

20. 888, 448, 228, 118, _____ , _____ , _____

Number Patterns ANSWER KEY

1. 150, 200, 250, 300, **350, 400,450**   (+ 50)

2. 1, 7, 49, 343, **2401, 16807, 117649**   (x 7)

3. 654, 641, 628, 615, **602, 589, 576**   (– 13)

4. 13312, 3328, 832, 208, **52, 13, 3.25** (÷ 4)

5. 72, 78, 84, 90, **96, 102, 108**   (+ 6)

6. 23, 27.5, 32, 36.5, **41, 45.5, 50**   (+ 4.5)

7. 123, 234, 345, 456, **567, 678, 789**

    drop the first number, add the next consecutive counting number
    on the end

8. 115, 105, 96, 88, **81, 75, 70**   (– 10, – 9, – 8, – 7 ...)

9. 86, 84, 80, 74, **66, 56, 44**   (– 2, – 4, – 6, – 8, – 10 ...)

10. 2, 3, 4.5, 6.75, **10.125, 15.1875, 22.78125** (x 1.5)

11. 99, 98, 96, 93, **89, 84, 78**   (– 1, –2, – 3, – 4, – 5 ...)

12. 11, 43, 75, 107, **139, 171, 203**   (+ 32)

13. 2, 5, 11, 20, **32, 47, 65**   (+ 3, + 6, + 9, + 12)

14. 842, 759, 676, 593, **510, 427, 344**   (– 83)

15. 1, 2, 4, 7, **11, 16, 22**   (+ 1, +2, +3, +4, +5)

16. 5, 16, 38, 82, **170, 346, 698**   (+ 3 then x 2)

17. 12, 18, 27, 40.5, **60.75, 91.125, 136.6875**   (÷ 2 then + the
                                                     original number)

18. 2, 3, 5, 8, 13, **21, 34, 55**   (add the two previous
                                             numbers together)

19. 4, 13, 40, 121, **364, 1093, 3280**   (x 3 then + 1)

20. 888, 448, 228, 118, **63, 35.5, 21.75** (÷ 2 then + 4)

© Substitute Teacher Training Institute

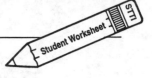

Calendar Math

1995

S M T W T F S								**S M T W T F S**								**S M T W T F S**								**S M T W T F S**		

JANUARY
```
S  M  T  W  T  F  S
1  2  3  4  5  6  7
8  9 10 11 12 13 14
15 16 17 18 19 20 21
22 23 24 25 26 27 28
29 30 31
```

FEBRUARY
```
S  M  T  W  T  F  S
            1  2  3  4
5  6  7  8  9 10 11
12 13 14 15 16 17 18
19 20 21 22 23 24 25
26 27 28
```

MARCH
```
S  M  T  W  T  F  S
            1  2  3  4
5  6  7  8  9 10 11
12 13 14 15 16 17 18
19 20 21 22 23 24 25
26 27 28 29 30 31
```

APRIL
```
S  M  T  W  T  F  S
                     1
2  3  4  5  6  7  8
9 10 11 12 13 14 15
16 17 18 19 20 21 22
23 24 25 26 27 28 29
30
```

MAY
```
S  M  T  W  T  F  S
   1  2  3  4  5  6
7  8  9 10 11 12 13
14 15 16 17 18 19 20
21 22 23 24 25 26 27
28 29 30 31
```

JUNE
```
S  M  T  W  T  F  S
             1  2  3
4  5  6  7  8  9 10
11 12 13 14 15 16 17
18 19 20 21 22 23 24
25 26 27 28 29 30
```

JULY
```
S  M  T  W  T  F  S
                     1
2  3  4  5  6  7  8
9 10 11 12 13 14 15
16 17 18 19 20 21 22
23 24 25 26 27 28 29
30 31
```

AUGUST
```
S  M  T  W  T  F  S
       1  2  3  4  5
6  7  8  9 10 11 12
13 14 15 16 17 18 19
20 21 22 23 24 25 26
27 28 29 30 31
```

SEPTEMBER
```
S  M  T  W  T  F  S
                  1  2
3  4  5  6  7  8  9
10 11 12 13 14 15 16
17 18 19 20 21 22 23
24 25 26 27 28 29 30
```

OCTOBER
```
S  M  T  W  T  F  S
1  2  3  4  5  6  7
8  9 10 11 12 13 14
15 16 17 18 19 20 21
22 23 24 25 26 27 28
29 30 31
```

NOVEMBER
```
S  M  T  W  T  F  S
            1  2  3  4
5  6  7  8  9 10 11
12 13 14 15 16 17 18
19 20 21 22 23 24 25
26 27 28 29 30
```

DECEMBER
```
S  M  T  W  T  F  S
                  1  2
3  4  5  6  7  8  9
10 11 12 13 14 15 16
17 18 19 20 21 22 23
24 25 26 27 28 29 30
31
```

1. How many days are there between March 5th and October 30th? _____

2. How many months have names with four or less letters in their name? _____

3. How many days are in these "short name" months combined? _____

4. How days are there in the month you were born? _____

5. State laws require that there are 180 days in a school year. If school started on August 15 and you went seven days a week without any days off for holidays or weekends, when would summer vacation begin? _____

6. Suppose there was a law that only allowed you to attend school on odd numbered dates, Monday through Friday. How many days would you attend school in the month of October? _____

7. There are 24 hours in one day. How many hours are there in the month of June? _____

8. There are 365 days in a year (excluding leap year). Figure out, as of today, how many days old you are. _____

9.   Which months have 30 days? | Which have 31 days?

    _____   _____ | _____   _____

    _____   _____ | _____   _____

    _____   _____ | _____   _____

    _____   _____ | _____   _____

Calendar Math

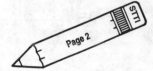

10. Which month did you not list in the previous question? _____

11. If you left on April 26th for a 14 day vacation to Hawaii, on what day would you return home? _____

12. How many school days are there between February 26 and April 19? _____

13. What year is your calendar? _____ What is something you remember from that year? _____

14. If school lets out for summer vacation on June 1 and begins again in the fall on August 28, how many days of summer vacation do you get? _____

15. How many Mondays are there in the month of October? _____

16. How many days are there between Christmas Day and New Years Day? _____

17. Do any months in your calendar have a Friday the 13th? _____ Which ones? _____

    _____

18. How many days are there between Valentine's Day and Independence Day? _____

19. Suppose you only went to school on Monday, Wednesday, and Friday. How many days would you go to school in the month of March? _____

20. Think up your own Calendar Math question and have someone else solve it.

    Question: _____

    _____

    Answer: _____

© Substitute Teacher Training Institute

Calendar Math ANSWER KEY

1.   238 days

2.   3 months

3.   92 days

4.   answers will vary

5.   February 10

6.   11 days

7.   720 hours

8.   answers will vary

9.   30 Days: April, June, September, November / 31 Days: January, March, May, July, August, October, December

10. February

11. May 9

12. 37 days

13. 1995; answers will vary

14. 87 days

15. 5 Mondays

16. 6 days

17. Yes; January & October

18. 139 days

19. 14 days

20. answers will vary

Name that Musical

Time: 30 minutes

Objective: Students will attempt to identify famous stage musicals from information about the music they are best-known for.

Materials Needed: pencils, paper, Musical Information (see below)

Advance Preparation: none

Procedure:

1. Divide the class into small groups.
2. Explain that in this activity you (the teacher) will read some information about a famous stage musical. As a group, they will have two minutes to determine and write down the name of the musical you have described. At the end of the two minute discussion time, each group holds up a piece of paper with the name of a musical on it. If the name is correct, the group gets two points, if it is close, but not quite right, one point may be awarded.
3. Play continues until all of the musicals have been described.
4. Additional information about the musical such as the story line, may be provided by the teacher, to help students identify it, as is appropriate.
5. The group with the most points at the end wins.

Musical Information

This musical was first performed in New York, 1946. The music and lyrics were both written by Irving Berlin. Best-known songs include, *There's No Business Like Show Business*, and *Anything You Can Do I Can Do Better*. What is the title of this musical production? (*Annie Get Your Gun*)

This musical was first performed in London, 1978. The music was written by Andrew Lloyd-Webber, with lyrics by Tim Rice. Best-known songs include, *Don't Cry For Me Argentina*. What is the title of this musical production? *(Evita)*

This musical was first performed in New York, 1946. The music was written by Jim Jacobs, with lyrics by Warren Casey. Best-known songs include, *Summer Nights*. What is the title of this musical production? *(Grease)*

This musical was first performed in New York, 1950. The music and lyrics were both written by Frank Loesser. Best-known songs include, *Luck Be A Lady*, *if I Were A Bell*, and *Sit Down You're Rocking The Boat*. What is the title of this musical production? *(Guys and Dolls)*

This musical was first performed in New York, 1957. The music was written by Leonard Bernstein with lyrics by Stephen Sondheim. Best-known songs include, *Maria*, *Tonight*, *America*, and *I Feel Pretty*. What is the title of this musical production? *(West Side Story)*

This musical was first performed in New York, 1956. The music was written by Frederick Loewe with lyrics by Alan Jay Lerner. Best-known songs include, *The Rain in Spain*, *On The Street Where You Live*, and *I Could Have Danced All Night*. What is the title of this musical production? *(My Fair Lady)*

This musical was first performed in New York, 1959. The music was written by Richard Rodgers with lyrics by Oscar Hammerstein. Best-known songs include, *My Favorite Things* and *Climb Every Mountain*. What is the title of this musical production? *(The Sound of Music)*

Teacher Directed Lesson

This musical was first performed in New York, 1967. The music was written by Galt MacDermot, with lyrics by Gerome Ragni and James Rado. Best-known songs include, *Aquarius*. What is the title of this musical production? *(Hair)*

This musical was first performed in New York, 1927. The music was written by Jerome Kern with lyrics by Oscar Hammerstein. Best-known songs include, *Old Man River*, and *Why Do I Love You*. What is the title of this musical production? *(Show Boat)*

This musical was first performed in New York, 1951. The music was written by Richard Rodgers and Oscar Hammerstein. Best-known songs include, *I Whistle A Happy Tune*. What is the name of this musical production? *(The King and I)*

This musical was first performed in New York, 1943. The music was written by Richard Rodgers and Oscar Hammerstein. Best-known songs include, *Oh What A Beautiful Morning* and *The Surrey With The Fringe On Top*. What is the name of this musical production? *(Oklahoma)*

This musical was first performed in New York, 1949. The music was written by Richard Rodgers and Oscar Hammerstein. Best-known songs include, *Some Enchanted Evening* and *I'm Gonna Wash That Man Right Out Of My Hair*. What is the name of this musical production? *(South Pacific)*

This musical was first performed in New York, 1945. The music was written by Richard Rodgers and Oscar Hammerstein. Best-known songs include, *June Is Busting Out All Over*. What is the name of this musical production. *(Carousel)*

© Substitute Teacher Training Institute

Musical Terms

Match the musical terms below with the correct definition on the right.

_____ 1. Concerto

_____ 2. Overture

_____ 3. Suite

_____ 4. Chamber Music

_____ 5. Choral Music

_____ 6. Ballet

_____ 7. Folksong

_____ 8. Quartet

_____ 9. Theme

_____ 10. Variations

_____ 11. Waltz

_____ 12. Requiem

_____ 13. Movement

_____ 14. Aubade

_____ 15. Chanterelle

A. singing on a grand scale often complete with massive choirs and orchestras

B. a musical composition in honor of the dead

C. the repetition of a theme with changes in rhythm or style

D. a long piece of music played by a solo performer and accompanied by a symphony orchestra

E. music to be played in the morning, perhaps to awaken someone

F. a dance rhythm of one strong beat followed by two lesser beats

G. short orchestral piece designed to precede and set the mood for an opera or play

H. a group of pieces either played separately one after the other or as one continuous piece of music

I. the main melody of a musical work

J. a traditional song, composer unknown, passed from one generation to the next

K. a section of a larger musical work with a distinct beginning and end

L. the name given to the highest string on any bowed instrument

M. a type of classical music played by small groups of musicians without any singing

N. a piece of music written for four musicians

O. an art form that uses dancing, scenery, and music to tell a story

Musical Terms ANSWER KEY

1. Concerto   D.   a long piece of music played by a solo performer and accompanied by a symphony orchestra

2. Overture   G.   short orchestral piece designed to precede and set the mood for an opera or play

3. Suite   H.   a group of pieces either played separately one after the other or as one continuous piece of music

4. Chamber Music   M.   a type of classical music played by small groups of musicians without any singing

5. Choral Music   A.   singing on a grand scale often complete with massive choirs and orchestras

6. Ballet   O.   an art form that uses dancing, scenery, and music to tell a story

7. Folksong   J.   a traditional song, composer unknown, passed from one generation to the next

8. Quartet   N.   a piece of music written for four musicians

9. Theme   I.   the main melody of a musical work

10. Variations   C.   the repetition of a theme with changes in rhythm or style

11. Waltz   F.   a dance rhythm of one strong beat followed by two lesser beats

12. Requiem   B.   a musical composition in honor of the dead

13. Movement   K.   a section of a larger musical work with a distinct beginning and end

14. Aubade   E.   music to be played in the morning, perhaps to awaken someone

15. Chanterelle   L.   the name given to the highest string on any bowed instrument

© Substitute Teacher Training Institute

Musical Directions

How well do you know your musical directions? The Italian terms below are often used to indicate the tempo, style, or expression with which a composition is to be played. How many can you match with the correct interpretation on the right?

_____ 1. Adagio	A. Get softer
_____ 2. Allegro	B. Whispered
_____ 3. Andante	C. Majestically
_____ 4. Crescendo	D. Pluck the string
_____ 5. Diminuendo	E. Repeat the note(s) rapidly (literally "trembling")
_____ 6. Forte	F. Moderately soft
_____ 7. Fortissimo	G. Medium Speed (literally "at a walking pace")
_____ 8. Largo	H. Short, detached notes
_____ 9. Legato	I. Fast
_____10. Maestoso	J. Play again from the start
_____11. Mezzo Forte	K. Smoothly, with long notes
_____12. Mezzo Piano	L. Loud
_____13. Pianissimo	M. Get slower
_____14. Pizzicato	N. Moderately loud
_____15. Prestissimo	O. Very, very fast
_____16. Presto	P. Slow
_____17. Staccato	Q. Get Louder
_____18. Vivace	R. Very loud
_____19. Sotto Voce	S. Slow
_____20. Ritardando	T. Very soft
_____21. Con Brio	U. Play with sliding notes
_____22. Da Capo	V. Soft
_____23. Glissando	W. Lively
_____24. Piano	X. Very fast
_____25. Tremolo	Y. Spirited

Musical Directions ANSWER KEY

1.	Adagio	P.	Slow
2.	Allegro	I.	Fast
3.	Andante	G.	Medium Speed (literally "at a walking pace")
4.	Crescendo	Q.	Get Louder
5.	Diminuendo	A.	Get softer
6.	Forte	L.	Loud
7.	Fortissimo	R.	Very loud
8.	Largo	S.	Slow
9.	Legato	K.	Smoothly, with long notes
10.	Maestoso	C.	Majestically
11.	Mezzo Forte	N.	Moderately loud
12.	Mezzo Piano	F.	Moderately soft
13.	Pianissimo	T.	Very soft
14.	Pizzicato	D.	Pluck the string
15.	Prestissimo	O.	Very, very fast
16.	Presto	X.	Very fast
17.	Staccato	H.	Short, detached notes
18.	Vivace	W.	Lively
19.	Sotto Voce	B.	Whispered
20.	Ritardando	M.	Get slower
21.	Con Brio	Y.	Spirited
22.	Da Capo	J.	Play again from the start
23.	Glissando	U.	Play with sliding notes
24.	Piano	V.	Soft
25.	Tremolo	E.	Repeat the note(s) rapidly (literally "trembling")

© Substitute Teacher Training Institute

NAME _____

Music Makers

Match the famous music makers below with their description on the right.

_____ 1. Louis Armstrong

_____ 2. Beach Boys

_____ 3. Beatles

_____ 4. Johnny Cash

_____ 5. Ray Charles

_____ 6. Bob Dylan

_____ 7. Michael Jackson

_____ 8. Scott Joplin

_____ 9. Andrew Lloyd-Webber

_____ 10. Glen Miller

_____ 11. Elvis Presley

_____ 12. Diana Ross

_____ 13. John Philip Sousa

_____ 14. Cole Porter

_____ 15. Stradivarius

A. American country singer whose songs are often based on the folklore of the American West.

B. Latin name of a famous Italian family of violin makers.

C. American popular singer whose real name is Robert Zimmerman. He pioneered the folk-rock style in the mid-1960's.

D. American band leader of World War II known mainly for his theme tune, *Moonlight Serenade*.

E. American songwriter, renowned for his catchy tunes and witty lyrics, such as *Anything Goes* and *Your The Top*.

F. American ragtime composer best known for writing *The Entertainer* and *Maple Leaf Rag*.

G. American popular singer who rose to fame with her group, the *Supremes*, in 1964 before becoming a solo singer and actress.

H. American popular singer and organist, blind from the age of six, who pioneered soul music with hits like, *Georgia On My Mind*.

I. British rock group first formed in 1956 as *The Quarrymen*, after tremendous success with hits like, *A Hard Day's Night*, they broke up in 1970.

J. American jazz trumpeter and singer, who founded the solo style of improvisation in jazz in the 1920's.

K. British composer of musicals which include *Evita*, *The Phantom of the Opera*, and *Cats*.

L. American singer who was the most popular rock and roll star of the 1950's.

M. American band leader and composer most remembered for his many famous marches.

N. American pop singer who rose to fame as a boy in a family group. His albums include *Off The Wall* and *Thriller*.

O. American rock group formed in 1961, whose albums include *Surfin' USA*.

Utah State University

163

Music Makers ANSWER KEY

1. Louis Armstrong   J. American jazz trumpeter and singer, who founded the solo style of improvisation in jazz in the 1920's.

2. Beach Boys   O. American rock group formed in 1961, whose albums include *Surfin' USA*.

3. Beatles   I. British rock group first formed in 1956 as *The Quarrymen*, after tremendous success with hits like, *A Hard Days Night*, they broke up in 1970.

4. Johnny Cash   A. American country singer whose songs are often based on the folklore of the American West.

5. Ray Charles   H. American popular singer and organist, blind from the age of six, who pioneered soul music with hits like, *Georgia On My Mind*.

6. Bob Dylan   C. American popular singer whose real name is Robert Zimmerman. He pioneered the folk-rock style in the mid-1960s.

7. Michael Jackson   N. American pop singer who rose to fame as a boy in a family group. His albums include *Off The Wall* and *Thriller*.

8. Scott Joplin   F. American ragtime composer best known for writing *The Entertainer* and *Maple Leaf Rag*.

9. Andrew Lloyd-Webber   K. British composer of musicals which include *Evita*, *The Phantom of the Opera*, and *Cats*.

10. Glen Miller   D. American band leader of World War II known mainly for his theme tune, *Moonlight Serenade*.

11. Elvis Presley   L. American singer who was the most popular rock and roll star of the 1950's.

12. Diana Ross   G. American popular singer who rose to fame with her group, the *Supremes*, in 1964 before becoming a solo singer and actress.

13. John Philip Sousa   M. American band leader and composer most remembered for his many famous marches.

14. Cole Porter   E. American songwriter, renowned for his catchy tunes and witty lyrics, such as *Anything Goes* and *Your The Top*.

15. Stradivarius   B. Latin name of a famous Italian family of violin makers.

© Substitute Teacher Training Institute

Fascinating Facts About Famous Musicians

You probably know that Scott Joplin wrote *The Entertainer* and is considered the father of ragtime music, but did you know he didn't attend school until his teens, college until he was twenty-seven, and that when he died he was buried in an unmarked grave? Listed below are 10 famous musicians, a title of their work, and a fascinating fact about their life. Can you place the correct letter of their work and number of the fascinating fact about their life in the blanks before each musician?

_____ _____ Vivaldi

_____ _____ Bach

_____ _____ Mozart

_____ _____ Beethoven

_____ _____ Chopin

_____ _____ Brahms

_____ _____ Tchaikovsky

_____ _____ Gilbert & Sullivan

_____ _____ Stravinsky

_____ _____ Gershwin

A. The Magic Flute

B. Four Seasons

C. Minute Waltz

D. Brandenburg Concertos

E. The Pirates of Penzance

F. 1812 Overture

G. Moonlight Sonata

H. Rhapsody in Blue

I. The Rite of Spring

J. Lullaby and Goodnight

1. He once held his wife's hand during childbirth and with his other hand wrote music.

2. At age seven he begged for piano lessons, but playing the piano made him too excited to sleep.

3. He once composed forty-six pieces of music while spending a month in jail.

4. As a boy he played violin duets with his father at church.

5. When in a new city he always visited the zoo first.

6. When he died one out of ten people in Vienna came to pay their respects.

7. Though not friends, they collaborated, mostly by correspondence for 20 years on 14 operettas.

8. At age sixteen he left school to work 10 hours a day in a music store, by nineteen he was rich and famous

9. He kept his pockets filled with candy and little pictures to give to neighborhood children on his walks.

10. His practical jokes included putting people to sleep with soft music then waking them up with a bang.

Fascinating Facts About Famous Musicians ANSWER KEY

B.	4.	Vivaldi	Four Seasons	As a boy he played violin duets with his father at church.
D.	3.	Bach	Brandenburg Concertos	He once composed forty-six pieces of music while spending a month in jail.
A.	1.	Mozart	The Magic Flute	He once held his wife's hand during childbirth and with his other hand wrote music.
G.	6.	Beethoven	Moonlight Sonata	When he died one out of ten people in Vienna came to pay their respects.
C.	10.	Chopin	Minute Waltz	His practical jokes included putting people to sleep with soft music then waking them up with a bang.
J.	9.	Brahms	Lullaby and Goodnight	He kept his pockets filled with candy and little pictures to give to neighborhood children on his walks.
F.	2.	Tchaikovsky	1812 Overture	At age seven he begged for piano lessons, but playing the piano made him too excited to sleep.
E.	7.	Gilbert & Sullivan	The Pirates of Penzance	Though not friends, they collaborated, mostly by correspondence for 20 years on 14 operettas.
I.	5.	Stravinsky	The Rite of Spring	When in a new city he always visited the zoo first.
H.	8.	Gershwin	Rhapsody in Blue	At age sixteen he left school to work 10 hours a day in a music store, by nineteen he was rich and famous.

© Substitute Teacher Training Institute

Experiments, Tricks, and Activities

The activities in this section can be used in a number of different ways. With little, or no preparation they can fill an extra few minutes at the end of class or be presented as part of a comprehensive lesson. The information below provides insights and ideas for comprehensive lesson development.

The Learning Cycle

The Learning Cycle is a method of instruction which presents three types of activities in a specified order to accomplish effective learning. The three phases of the Learning Cycle are as follows:

1. **Exploration Phase:** Students explore what they already know about the topic. Questions are raised. Brainstorming and discovery activities are often used in this phase.

2. **Concept Development Phase:** This is the gaining new knowledge phase. Students learn the names of objects, events, and principles. Teacher explanations and student research is often part of gaining a general understanding of basic concepts during this phase.

3. **Concept Application Phase:** Students are asked to apply learned concepts to a new situation. The teacher poses a new problem or situation that can be solved on the basis of previous experiences. Posing a question, determining a possible answer, performing an experiment to verify the answer, and discussing the results is a common activity during the final phase.

The Scientific Method

The scientific method is a structured set of science procedures often used in scientific study. Students will most likely be familiar with the process, but it never hurts to review.

1. Identify a question or problem.
2. Gather relevant information.
3. Form a hypothesis (an educated guess about the solution or outcome of the problem).

4.   Test the hypothesis.

5.   Formulate results.

Often the results of one activity or experiment will lead to additional questions. By changing one of the variables and reworking the same basic experiment additional hypotheses can be tested.

Ideas for Stretching a Science Lesson

- Have students brainstorm related questions generated by the activity and discuss possible ways of finding the answers.

- Have students write step-by-step instructions for completing the activity portion of the lesson.

- Ask students to list five things that they learned from the lesson.

- Challenge students to write a short worksheet or quiz for the lesson and then exchange with each other.

- Assign students to write a creative story about how the world would be different if the scientific principle studied did not exist or was altered.

- Have students use their textbooks or other classroom resources to do further research on the topic and write a brief report.

By selecting a few activities, assembling needed materials, and developing class length lesson plans ahead of time, you will be prepared to successfully fill empty class time with exciting learning experiences.

The Slippery Bill

Equipment: A dollar bill or piece of paper measuring about three-by-five inches.

Procedure: Hold the bill horizontally in your left hand and get ready to catch it with your right thumb and fingers on each side of the bottom edge but not quite touching it. Drop the bill and catch it with your right hand. Easy! Now challenge a student to catch it, poised the same way you were, with thumb and fingers just off the bottom edge, while you hold the bill and release it. He will miss it almost every time.

Explanation: When you are both releasing and catching the bill, your brain signals your right hand to catch as it signals your left to release. When someone else is catching, he must rely on a visual clue before he begins to catch, and that almost always takes a little too long.

Not a Knot?

Equipment: Two or three feet of string.

Procedure: Lay the string out on a table. Hold one end in each hand, and pose the problem of how to tie a knot in it without letting go of either end.

Solution: Fold your arms, pick up each end, and unfold your arms. There will be a knot in the string because there was a "knot" in your arms.

Big Things in Small Holes

Equipment: A dime, a quarter, paper, and pencil.

Procedure: Trace around the dime on a small piece of paper and cut it out. Now challenge someone to put the quarter through the hole without tearing the paper.

Solution: With the quarter inside, fold the paper in half across the hole. Now just push the coin through. As long as the diameter of the coin is a bit less than half the circumference of the hole, it will go through easily.

White Light

Equipment: A shallow pan or bowl, a pocket mirror, and a flashlight.

Procedure: Fill the bowl with water and put the mirror halfway in at an angle of about 30 degrees to the surface of the water. Shine the flashlight at the mirror. A spectrum of colors will appear on the ceiling.

Explanation: This parallels Isaac Newton's experiment with a prism that proved the "white" sunlight to be made up of many colors. In this case, the water acts as a prism, refracting each wave length at a slightly different angle to form a rainbow on the ceiling. If there is direct sunlight in the room, set a glass of water in it and a spectrum of colors will appear on the windowsill.

To the Center

Equipment: A glass of water and a cork.

Procedure: Drop the cork in the glass of water. It will float to one side. Challenge someone to make the cork float in the center of the glass. If they are not able to—and the cork will probably head right back to the edge every time—carefully fill the glass with more water until it "bulges" over the top. The cork will move to the center.

Explanation: Surface tension creates the "bulge" and changes the surface of the water into a convex shape. The light cork floats to the center where the water is highest.

Boomerang Spinners

Equipment: Index cards and scissors.

Procedure: Cut a boomerang from an index card—A widespread V with legs about four inches long. Round all the corners slightly. Put the boomerang flat on a book with one leg projecting over the edge. Strike that projecting leg with a sharp forward motion of your pencil along the edge of the book. The boomerang will whirl up and away, then come back to you.

Explanation: The spinning of the boomerang makes it work like a gyroscope. While it spins, it maintains the same rotation plane. As it falls, the force of air on the now inclined blades pushes it back along its own path.

Chimes

Equipment: knife, fork, spoon, string, rubber bands

Procedure One: Tie the pieces of silverware at intervals on a length of the string so that they do not touch each other. Hold the ends of the string to the ears. As the head is moved the silver pieces will clang together and chimes can be heard.

Explanation: The sounds heard are very much like the sounds of ordinary clanking of the silver, except that each sound lasts longer since the silver is free to vibrate. The string conducts the sounds to the ears, making them louder and more mellow. The vibrations in the individual pieces are at regular frequencies and produce musical tones. Irregular vibrations would make noise.

Procedure Two: Replace the string with rubber bands tied together. Hold the rubber to the ears as the string was held. There will likely be no sound at all, certainly not chimes. This is because rubber is not elastic in the scientific sense.

Explanation: Vibrations from the silverware are fed into the string, and travel up the string to the ears. The string is elastic enough to transmit the vibrations with a little loss. In the rubber bands the sound energy is absorbed. The sound waves get weaker as they travel up and soon die out completely. The common definition of "elastic" is "stretchable-but-finally-coming-back." So in common usage a rubber band and things woven of rubber are elastic. In the scientific sense, glass and hard steel are very elastic, while rubber is not.

Lemon Fireworks

Equipment: a candle flame, lemon, and flour

Procedure One: Squeeze the lemon peel near the flame and small displays of "fireworks" may be seen shooting from the flame.

Explanation: As the lemon peel is bent, some of the oil and water in it squirt out into the flame. Some of the oil burns as it passes through the flame, and some of the water vaporizes and sputters.

Procedure Two: Sprinkle flour on the candle flame. Tiny sparkles will be seen as the flour particles catch fire. The particles must be fine, with a large part of their surfaces exposed to the oxygen of the air, to produce the effect.

The Rising Arms

Equipment: doorway

© Substitute Teacher Training Institute

Procedure: Stand in the doorway with hands resting at side. Press outward against the door frame, with the backs of your hands, as if trying to raise your arms. Slowly count to 25. Step away from the door frame and arms will begin to rise mysteriously.

Explanation: This is an example of the workings of mind and muscle. The count to 25 is sufficient to produce a persistent attempt to raise the arms. The door frame prevents this, but as soon as you step out of the doorway, the persistent effort to raise the arms becomes a possible reality.

The Goofy Ping-Pong Ball

Equipment: ping-pong ball, hard rubber comb, and a piece of wool cloth

Procedure: Rub the comb briskly against the cloth. Move it in circles around the ping-pong ball, it is not necessary to touch the ball. The ball will follow the comb.

Explanation: Rubbing places a charge of static electricity on the comb. The uncharged ball is attracted by the charge on the comb.

Getting a Rise

Equipment: sheet of paper and two books

Procedure: Suspend the paper by placing the books under each end. Blow straight under the paper, and it will bend downward, not upward as expected.

Explanation: Air in motion exerts less lateral or side pressure than air at rest or moving more slowly. When air is blown under the paper, it exerts less pressure than the still air above it. The still air then pushes the paper down. This is the principle by which airplanes fly.

Science Fact and Fiction

Science fiction writers love to predict the future. It seems impossible that many things described in today's science fiction will ever become a reality. However, many things that science fiction writer of long ago wrote about really do exist today. Can you guess the year when the inventions of science fiction writers actually became a reality?

Year	Invention	Predicted By
_____	1. Air-conditioned skyscrapers	Jules Verne, *In the Twenty-Ninth Century — The Day of an American Journalist* (1875)
_____	2. Artificial Intelligence (computers that can think for themselves)	Aaron Nadel, *The Thought Machine* (1927)
_____	3. Atomic Energy	H.G. Wells, *The World Set Free* (1914)
_____	4. Charge Cards	Edward Bellamy, *Looking Backward, 2000-1887* (1888)
_____	5. Lasers	Sir Francis Bacon (1626)
_____	6. Long-distance Submarines	Jules Verne, *Twenty Thousand Leagues Under the Sea* (1870)
_____	7. Microfilm	Hugo Gernsback, *Ralph 125C 41+* (1911)
_____	8. Navigational Satellites	Edward Everett Hale (1870)
_____	9. News Broadcasts	Jules Verne, *In the Twenty-Ninth Century* (1875)
_____	10. Robots	Karel Capek, *R. U. R. (Rossum's Universal Robots)* (1921)
_____	11. Space suits	Frank R. Paul, *Amazing Stories Magazine* (1939)
_____	12. Spacecraft that carry people to the Moon	Jules Verne, *From the Earth to the Moon* (1865) H.G. Wells, *The First Men in the Moon* (1901)
_____	13. Tape Recorders	Hugo Gernsback, *Ralph 125C 41+* (1911)
_____	14. Television	Jules Verne, *In the Twenty-Ninth Century* (1875) H.G. Wells, *The Time Machine* (1895)
_____	15. Test-tube Babies	Aldous Huxley, *Brave New World* (1931)

© Substitute Teacher Training Institute

Science Fact and Fiction ANSWER KEY

	Invention	Predicted By
1930	1. Air-conditioned skyscrapers	Jules Verne, *In the Twenty-Ninth Century — The Day of an American Journalist* (1875)
1950+	2. Artificial Intelligence	Aaron Nadel, *The Thought Machine* (1927)
1942	3. Atomic Energy	H.G. Wells, *The World Set Free* (1914)
1952	4. Charge Cards	Edward Bellamy, *Looking Backward, 2000-1887* (1888)
1960	5. Lasers	Sir Francis Bacon (1626)
1950+	6. Long-distance Submarines	Jules Verne, *Twenty Thousand Leagues Under the Sea* (1870)
1920	7. Microfilm	Hugo Gernsback, *Ralph 125C 41+* (1911)
1959	8. Navigational Satellites	Edward Everett Hale (1870)
1920	9. News Broadcasts	Jules Verne, *In the Twenty-Ninth Century* (1875)
1920+	10. Robots	Karel Capek, *R. U. R. (Rossum's Universal Robots)* (1921)
1950-1960's	11. Space suits	Frank R. Paul, *Amazing Stories* Magazine (1939)
1960	12. Spacecraft that could carry people to the Moon	Jules Verne, *From the Earth to the Moon* (1865) H.G. Wells, *The First Men in the Moon* (1901)
1936	13. Tape Recorders	Hugo Gernsback, *Ralph 124C 41+* (1911)
1920's	14. Television	Jules Verne, *In the Twenty-Ninth Century* (1875) H.G. Wells, *The Time Machine* (1895)
1978	15. Test-tube Babies	Aldous Huxley, *Brave New World* (1931)

Extension: Have students compute the number of years between the science fiction prediction and the actual invention.

Scientist Profile

Do you fit the profile of a scientist? Does science fit anywhere in your future career plans? Read the information below, following the directions as you go. The answers to these questions just might surprise you.

The Scientist Profile

As you read about the characteristics of scientists, put a star next to the personality traits you identify with.

Persistence   Persistence is not giving up. Scientists try to find answers to questions and then try and try again when attempted answers don't work out. A classic example is Paul Ehrlich, who tried 605 different drugs as cure for syphilis before he found "606" which worked. Today, the development of a new drug may require the screening of thousands of candidates.

Curiosity   Curiosity is the ability to be forever asking questions and then seeking the answers. The willingness to try out new ideas is an aspect of curiosity that is essential to science, for both research and teaching scientists.

Precision   Science often requires a steady, and precise hand for manipulating tiny objects in activities such as dissecting cells or repairing electronic equipment. Scientists also need a precise mind for noting fine distinctions and avoiding subtle errors.

Intelligence   Any scientist will find mental alertness, quickness, and agility useful in achieving success, but genius is not absolutely necessary. Some intelligence is essential, but flexible thinking skills are often more important than IQ points.

Objectivity & Honesty   Scientists must have a high regard for truth. Objectivity involves not deceiving oneself, and keeping an open mind to other possibilities even after a conclusion has been drawn. A scientist can not let enchantment with their ideas, laziness, or haste, keep them from checking and re-checking their ideas with experiment after experiment.

Social Skills   The ability to communicate ideas and work well with others. Most science specialties require individuals to work together as a team to produce the end product.

Writing Skills   Scientists are forever taking down information and preparing written materials which they share with others. The ability to record information accurately and communicate ideas clearly is an important aspect of scientific work.

Personality Types

Realistic   Interested in mechanical and physical activities; a tool-user, not socially skilled or sensitive.

Investigative   Interested in thinking, organizing and understanding; analytical, intellectual, curious, reserved, and scientific, not persuasive or social.

Social   Interested in helping, teaching, and serving others, friendly, cooperative, and tactful, not mechanical or technical.

Conventional   Interested in orderly, structured situations with clear guidelines; precise, accurate, clerical, and conforming.

© Substitute Teacher Training Institute

Enterprising   Interested in organizing, directing, persuading, and exercising authority; persuasive, ambitious, and optimistic; a leader.

Artistic   Interested in performing; emotional, autonomous, unconventional, impulsive and imaginative.

Scientists in general must be strongly investigative, but many research scientists are often artistic as well. Social scientists and teachers need to be social. The heads of laboratories, academic department heads, and managers need enterprising personality traits. Engineers are often investigative and realistic. Mathematicians need to be investigative, conventional, and sometimes artistic. Technicians are usually realistic and conventional.

1. Which personality type/types do you think best represents your personality? _____

2. According to the paragraph, what kind of career might be best suited to your personality type? _____

3. What personal traits and characteristics do you possess that would contribute to your success in this field of work?

_____

_____

_____

Fields of Science

Select the field of science below that you think you would enjoy working in the most.

Helping Sciences   Nurses, doctors, social workers, counselors, and other individuals who "help" other individual members of society during times of crisis or illness.

Social Sciences   Deal mostly with people as groups, instead of individually. Their work takes a look at the "big picture" and long term outcomes. The goal of the social sciences is to explain and influence how groups of people behave.

Life Sciences   The work of the life sciences is to understand the phenomena of life. How and what makes living things "tick," as well as the influence that non living things (drugs, temperature, food, stress, etc.) have on life. There is a branch of life science to study everything living on the planet.

Physical Sciences   The study of non-living matter. The formation of different materials, as well as their characteristics and how they interact with one another. Chemistry and physics are two of the major branches of the physical sciences.

Earth Sciences   Deal primarily with the study of the Earth. Geologists study the structure and history of the planet. Oceanography focuses on ocean traits and characteristics, while meteorology examines the weather atmosphere surrounding the earth.

Space Sciences   The two main branches of space science are astronomy, the study of stars and planets, and astrophysics, which strives to understand cosmic events in space. Future space science fields may include planetary engineers to make other planets livable and extraterrestrial anthropology.

Engineering   Engineers are the builders and makers of our society. They design and oversee construction of many things including cars, spacecraft, buildings, synthetic materials, and new breeds of plants.

1. Now that you've evaluated your own personality traits and had a brief overview of the many fields of science write down at least one science related career, or field that you are interested in learning more about. _____

Buzz Line

Time: 10+ minutes

Objective: Students will observe the complexities of verbal communication.

Materials: The Story (see below)

Advance Preparation: None

Directions:

To illustrate the complexities of verbal communication, line up ten students. Give the first student the story below. Ask him or her to read the story, and then pass it on to the next student. Once a student begins retelling the story, he or she may not stop or ask or answer any questions. Let the process continue through student ten. When they are finished, let the last student explain the story as best he or she can to the class. Now read the original story aloud. The differences between the two stories are amazing. Discuss the elements involved in this type of communication process.

An interesting way to amplify the value of feedback, is to give the same story simultaneously to a second group of ten students. Allow the second group to confer as they go along by asking questions or clarifying points that were misunderstood. The second group will generally turn in a more complete and accurate version.

Develop your own ideas along this line to demonstrate how feedback is essential to a complete communication process.

The Story

The following events took place recently: Mr. Jones visited the lost city of the Incas in Ecuador. While touring the vast ruins of this city, he met a couple from Czechoslovakia. They were a married couple, the man being sixty years old and the woman in her late fifties. The lady was a professor of history. All her life she had worked to visit the ruins of the Inca Indians. Her cousin had loaned her the money, and she was to fulfill her lifelong dream. Last Christmas, Mr. Jones was in New York riding down Fifth Avenue. There he saw this marvelous couple crossing the street. He stopped and renewed an unusual friendship. Surely this proved the old adage, "How small a world this is!"

© Substitute Teacher Training Institute

Name Dropping

Time:	30+ minutes
Objective:	Students will use voice and gestures to capsulize a well-known personality.
Materials:	tape, names of famous people
Advance Preparation:	Copy the names of famous people onto sheets of paper.

Directions:

Place the students in groups of five or six people. The instructor tapes a name of a famous personality to the back of the first player in each group. The first player goes to the group and shows their back to the group. The group then tries to act out this name by imitating characteristics of this celebrity. This may be done by voice, gestures or poses. After the first player guesses the name on their back, another player goes to the instructor to have a name taped on.

The game continues until each student in the group has had a turn.

This activity helps the students capsulize a well-known personality, imitate characteristics through voice and gesture, and work together.

A Sampling of Famous People

Michael Jordan	John Wayne	Donald Trump	Dan Rather
Bill Clinton	Hillary Clinton	O.J. Simpson	Jeff Foxworthy
Madonna	Tom Cruise	Sandra Bullock	Oprah Winfrey
Princess Diana	Mickey Mouse	Will Smith	Jay Leno
Tiger Woods	Jim Carrie	Steve Young	Roseanne

Making an Announcement

Time: 30+ minutes

Objective: Students will practice making an announcement to a group of people.

Materials: none

Advance Preparation: none

Directions:

Assign each student to write a list of four school-related announcements which they will present to the class. Announcements can be fact or fiction, but remind students that they will have to deliver them in a serious and business like manner. Share some examples, and set a time limit (5-10 minutes) for completing this part of the lesson.

Randomly select students to exit the classroom, knock on the door, request permission to make an announcement, receive permission, and deliver the announcements they have prepared. Repeat this process until all members of the class have delivered their announcements.

Note: Applause after announcements is appropriate.

Example

Student exits the classroom and knocks on the door.

Teacher opens the door.

Student: Excuse me Mr./Ms._____, could I make some announcements to your class?

Teacher: Yes. Please come in.

Student: I have been asked to make the following announcements:

1.   The French Club wishes to announce their upcoming field trip to Paris next week. Please turn in permission slips at the office.

2.   The Calculus Social will be today after school. Remember to bring your graphing calculator.

3.   The media center will be closed to all students for the rest of the week.

4.   Due to lack of interest, this year's high school graduation has been cancelled.

Applause

An Occasional Speech

Time: 30+ minutes

Objective: Students will prepare and deliver an appropriate speech for
                         a specified occasion.

Materials: none

Advance Preparation: Prepare a scenario for the speech.

Directions:

Explain to students that different events call for different types of speeches. Share the scenario you have selected with the class and discuss the purpose or necessary elements of the speech. For example, does the speech need to persuade, share information, console, express appreciation, etc.

Allow students 10-15 minutes to prepare a short (3 minutes or less) speech for the designated occasion.

As time permits, allow volunteers, or select students at random, to share their speech with the class.

NOTE: Applause at the end of each speech is appropriate.

Possible Speech Scenarios:

1. An acceptance speech after winning a $1,000,000 sweepstakes contest.

2. A speech given by a city official to announce the construction of a new city park.

3. A speech announcing to employees the closing of the business where they work.

4. A speech to honor the contributions of professional athletes to society.

5. A speech to persuade the school board to only hold classes four days a week.

6. A speech to inform the student body about the dangers of cafeteria food.

7. A speech to announce the assassination of the president of the United States.

Classroom Commercial

Time: 30+ minutes

Objective: Students will prepare a brief presentation designed to sell a product.

Materials: common classroom objects

Advance Preparation: none

Directions:

Arrange students in cooperative learning groups. Explain that each group will be assigned a classroom object and have 15 minutes to prepare a commercial or sales presentation for the object. The goal of the presentation is to convince fellow classmates that they must have one of the objects to be successful, popular, or survive at school.

Assign and distribute a different classroom object to each group of students. Allow students to use the object as a prop in their presentation. Remind students of the preparation time limit.

Have student groups take turns presenting their presentation/commercial before the class.

If time permits, discuss well known advertising or promotion campaign strategies that were imitated in the student presentations.

NOTE: Applause at the end of each presentation is appropriate.

Classroom Object Ideas

desk	backpack	chair	pencil sharpener
pencil	chalk	tape	calculator
eraser	pen	stapler	teacher's edition of class textbook

          © Substitute Teacher Training Institute

Are You a Good Listener

Attitudes	Almost Always	Usually	Some Times	Seldom	Almost Never
1. Do you like to listen to other people talk?	5	4	3	2	1
2. Do you encourage others to talk?	5	4	3	2	1
3. Do you listen even if you do not like the person who is talking?	5	4	3	2	1
4. Do you listen with equal interest whether the person talking is man or woman, young or old?	5	4	3	2	1
5. Do you listen with equal interest to a friend, acquaintance or stranger?	5	4	3	2	1
6. Do you put what you have been doing out of sight and out of mind?	5	4	3	2	1
7. Do you look at the speaker?	5	4	3	2	1
8. Do you ignore distractions?	5	4	3	2	1
9. Do you smile, nod your head, and otherwise encourage the speaker?	5	4	3	2	1
10. Do you think about what they are saying?	5	4	3	2	1
11. Do you try to figure out what they mean?	5	4	3	2	1
12. Do you try to figure out why they are saying it?	5	4	3	2	1
13. Do you let them finish what they are trying to say?	5	4	3	2	1
14. If they hesitate, do you encourage them to go on?	5	4	3	2	1
15. Do you restate what they said and ask them if you got it right?	5	4	3	2	1

Add up your listening points, then compare your points to the scale below.

75-70 Excellent Listener: Keep up the good work!

69-55 Good Listener: Identify skills to work on (4 or lower) .

54-34 Fair Listener: Conscious effort on your part will greatly improve your listening skills.

33-15 Poor Listener: Identify your weakest listening skills and work on them.

NAME _____

Listening

Directions:

1. In the space provided to the left of each statement write the letter of the item that best completes the sentence.

2. Check you answers with the key found at the end of the questions.

3. Write a brief paragraph about how you could incorporate something you learned from this activity into a presentation to increase its effectiveness.

_____ 1. **Hearing refers to:**
    (a) the reception of sounds   (c) mentally sorting out meanings
    (b) the interpretation of sounds   (d) 1/2 of the communication process

_____ 2. **The average person misses _____ percent of what they hear.**
    (a) 10   (c) 50
    (b) 25   (d) 75

_____ 3. **Average listening speed is approximately _____ the average speaking rate.**
    (a) one-half   (c) twice
    (b) equal to   (d) ten times

_____ 4. **Listening barriers do not include:**
    (a) ordinary noise   (c) distractions that come from within the listener
    (b) distractions that come from the speaker   (d) attempts to evaluate the speech from the speaker

_____ 5. **Open-minded listening means:**
    (a) listening with no opinions   (c) agreeing with the speaker
    (b) keeping one's opinions open   (d) being indecisive

_____ 6. **The source of a message means:**
    (a) the listener   (c) the ideas of the speaker
    (b) the speaker   (d) the introductory remarks

_____ 7. **An important step in listening is:**
    (a) providing positive feedback   (c) concentrating on non-verbal listening
    (b) making use of association   (d) all of the above

_____ 8. **The most extreme example of being closed-minded is:**
    (a) speaking too much when on the telephone   (c) not allowing the other person to ask talking questions during an interview
    (b) monopolizing a group discussion   (d) not being willing to hear an opponent's arguments

_____ 9. **As part of a captive audience listening to a boring speaker, you can benefit most from trying to:**
    (a) focus on the speaker's non-verbal communication   (c) ignore the speaker
    (b) apply the message   (d) fake interest and attention to yourself

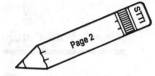

10. Looking a speaker directly in the eyes is a form of:

(a) closed-minded listening

(b) a listening barrier

(c) a memory aid

(d) positive feedback

11. Listening for central ideas means listening for:

(a) statistics

(b) stories

(c) main points

(d) examples

12. Listening for central ideas is often most difficult when listening to:

(a) a play

(b) a speech

(c) a conversation

(d) an oral reading

13. Association is:

(a) a form of feedback

(b) a kind of memory aid

(c) a type of speech listening

(d) one aspect of non-verbal listening

14. A speaker who uses "cardstacking" presents the audience with:

(a) all the facts

(b) only facts that support the speaker

(c) only facts that will appeal to the audience

(d) visual aids such as charts and graphs

15. A glittering generality is a word or phrase that:

(a) few people will agree with

(b) most audiences will applaud

(c) is vague and undefined

(d) gives a speech spark

16. A testimonial involves:

(a) a person's will

(b) a celebrity's opinion

(c) courtroom evidence

(d) the result of police interrogation on a subject

17. Begging the question refers to:

(a) asking the judge for mercy

(b) asking for evidence

(c) failing to stick to one's ideas

(d) failing to prove a point

18. The term non-sequitur means that:

(a) the speech is not appropriate

(b) the speaker is hiding something

(c) the evidence given does not support the claim

(d) the audience cannot be expected to agree with the speaker's argument

19. An awareness of paralanguage is important in:

(a) applying the message to oneself

(b) making use of association

(c) evaluating non-verbal communication

(d) overlooking speech impediment

20. Non-verbal communication includes:

(a) everything except his appearance

(b) everything about a speaker

(c) everything about a speaker except the words

(d) everything he says and does except his movements

ANSWER KEY

1. A 2. D 3. C 4. D 5. B 6. B 7. D 8. D 9. B 10. D

11. C 12. C 13. B 14. B 15. C 16. D 17. D 18. C 19. C 20. C

Asking Questions

Time: 30 minutes

Objective: Students will learn the importance of asking questions in order to achieve what they really want.

Materials: 4 gift wrapped boxes, 2 candy bars or other wrapped candy, *Ask Me a Question* worksheet

Advance Preparation: photocopy student worksheets, wrap boxes

Procedure:

1. Display two of the boxes in front of the class. One should be attractively wrapped and have inside a piece of candy, the other should be unattractive (perhaps wrapped in torn newspaper held together with masking tape) and have nothing inside.

2. Select one student to come to the front of the room. Explain that they can choose one of the boxes and keep whatever is inside. Do not encourage the student to ask questions or take a lot of time deciding, urge them to hurry and make a quick decision. Students will invariably choose the unattractive empty box.

3. Have the student open the box of their choice and show contents, or lack there of, to the rest of the class.

4. Explain that making decisions about future school, and career plans can be a lot like selecting a gift wrapped box. You can either make a quick decision and hope for the best, or you can ask a lot of questions to try and find out if you are getting what you really want. (At this point you may want to unwrap the other box and show the candy that was inside.)

5. Explain that the worksheet they are about to complete is designed to help them start thinking about their future and what it is they really want.

6. Have students complete the *Ask Me a Question* worksheet.

7. As a concluding activity display the other two wrapped boxes, one with candy inside and the other empty. Select another student to come to the front of the room and select one of the boxes. Hopefully they will take the time to ask questions and get the one they really want.

NAME _____

Ask Me a Question

1. Ten years from now, where would you like to be living?   (small town, city, country, desert, specific state, etc.)
_____

2. How much training or schooling are you willing to get in preparation for an occupation?   (on the job training, vocational training, college degree, etc.) _____

3. What kind of hobbies or after work activities do you want to be able to participate in?_____
_____

4. What kind of an environment do you want to work in?   (quiet, busy, social, high-tech, etc.) _____
_____

5. What type of clothes do you want to wear to work every day?_____

On the lines below mark the location which you think best describes your position and preferences .

6. I would rather work with:

people	_____	things
objects	_____	ideas
new people every day	_____	the same people every day
familiar equipment	_____	new technology

7. At work I would rather be:

outside	_____	inside
part of a team	_____	independent
supervised	_____	a supervisor
intellectually challenged	_____	physically challenged

8. Each day at work I would like to:

provide a service	_____	sell a product
follow a routine	_____	do something new

Rank the following job attributes from 1 to 5 (1 = not very important and 5 = very important), then circle the one you feel is most important to your job satisfaction.

9. social status of job	1	2	3	4	5
10. salary and benefits	1	2	3	4	5
11. working hours	1	2	3	4	5
12. opportunities for advancement	1	2	3	4	5
13. job security	1	2	3	4	5
14. seeing results	1	2	3	4	5
15. enjoying what you do	1	2	3	4	5

16. Write down the name of a career, job, or occupation, that you think is well suited to your interests and needs identified above. _____

17. If you were to interview a person who works at this job or in this field, what questions could you ask to find out if you are really suited to this type of work? _____
_____
_____

NAME _____

Career Dreams and Fantasies

1. In the columns below fill in the appropriate information about your career fantasies or dreams. Include even the briefest or wildest image or dream.

2. Include as fantasies or dreams both names of occupations (chef, pilot, teacher, etc.) and states of being (rich, famous, powerful, etc.)

3. Record information about any possible career fantasies/dreams that you can think of for the future.

Age	Career Fantasy/Dream	Reasons Chosen or Rewards
5	Astronaut	fly to the moon, wear space suits, float in space
7	Millionaire	buy toys, buy lots of candy
FUTURE		

Browse through your list of fantasies. Do you notice any common themes of interest, skills, or values? _____

_____

Browse through your list of reasons chosen and rewards. List one at least one job, occupation, or career, that would provide most of the rewards you are seeking. _____

NAME _____

Personal Preferences

1. Brainstorm 3 responses for each topic.

2. Put a star next to the response you prefer for each topic.

3. In the right hand column explain why you think you selected the one you did.

Brainstorming	**Explanation**
A. If I had a $50,000 gift to use in one day, or lose it, I would . . .	
1.	
2.	
3.	
B. It would make me happy to . . .	
1.	
2.	
3.	
C. If I could magically change anything in the world, I would . . .	
1.	
2.	
3.	

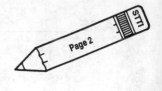
Personal Preferences

Brainstorming	**Explanation**

D. If I could be guaranteed success at anything I did,
    I would like to . . .

1.

2.

3.

E. Adjectives I would like others to describe me
    with are . . .

1.

2.

3.

F. If I could choose to spend the day with anyone,
    I would choose . . .

1.

2.

3.

What are the themes or repeated values in your responses?   (money, people, things, etc.)

_____

Which topic and responses do you feel most strongly about?

_____

List one thing you learned about yourself from this activity and how you can use this information to assist in making plans for your future. _____

_____

NAME _____

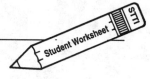

Interests, Skills, and Jobs

To the side of each item rank your INTEREST LEVEL in that item on a scale of 0 to 10, (0 = low interest, and 10 = high interest). Then add the numbers together to compute a total for each category.

Realistic

_____ Agriculture

_____ Pet Care

_____ Backpacking

_____ Simple Plumbing

_____ Electrical Repairs

Total = _____

Investigative

_____ Chemistry

_____ Physics

_____ Knowing how to put out a grease fire

_____ Converting to Metrics

_____ Using a Microscope

Total = _____

Artistic

_____ Desktop Publishing

_____ Journalism

_____ Music

_____ Drama

_____ Interior Design

Total = _____

Social

_____ Psychology

_____ Sociology

_____ History

_____ Counseling

_____ Teaching

Total = _____

Enterprising

_____ Marketing

_____ Political Science

_____ Public Relations

_____ Management

_____ Organizing a Project

Total = _____

Traditional

_____ Accounting

_____ Using Electronic Mail

_____ Information Systems

_____ Following Schedules

_____ Simple Calculations

Total = _____

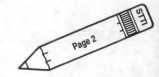

Interests, Skills, and Jobs

To the side of each item rank your SKILL LEVEL or ability for completing the item, when compared with the ability of others your own age. Rank you skill level on a scale of 0 to 10, (0 = low ability, and 10 = high ability) then add the numbers together to compute a total for each category.

Realistic

_____ understanding technology

_____ using tools

_____ driving all types of vehicles

_____ building things

_____ physically coordinated

Total = _____

Investigative

_____ abstract thinking

_____ experimenting

_____ analyzing facts

_____ visualizing solutions

_____ explaining how things work

Total = _____

Artistic

_____ using expressive language

_____ drawing or painting

_____ fashion conscious

_____ writing and spelling

_____ innovative/creative

Total = _____

Enterprising

_____ organizing a group

_____ persuasive

_____ optimistic

_____ diplomatic

_____ assertive/outgoing

Total = _____

Social

_____ communication

_____ listening to others

_____ working cooperatively

_____ showing empathy

_____ explaining things well

Total = _____

Traditional

_____ following routines and schedules

_____ managing finances

_____ calm/patient

_____ tactful/polite

_____ following through

Total = _____

Which category did you score the highest in the interest inventory? _____

Which category did you score the highest in the skills inventory? _____

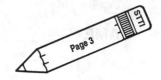

Interests, Skills, and Jobs

Study the occupations listed in these categories below.

Write down at least five occupations you are INTERESTED in. (They do not have to be occupations from the lists below.)

1.   4.

2.   5.

3.

Write down at least five occupations you already have some SKILLS in. (They do not have to be occupations from the lists below.)

1.   4.

2.   5.

3.

Write down at least three occupations you have both interest and skills in. (They do not have to be occupations from the lists below.)

1.   3.

2.

Write down at least one thing you could do within the next week to further explore or prepare for one of these three career opportunities. _____

Realistic	Investigative	Artistic	Social	Enterprising	Traditional
mechanic	dentist	actor	coach	construction contractor	cashier
chef	computer systems analyst	architect	teacher	bill collector	legal secretary
carpenter		artist	librarian		data entry clerk
fire fighter	aerospace engineer	interior designer	medical assistant	education administrator	medical record technician
equipment operator	conservationist	landscape architect	cosmetologist	lawyer	receptionist
electrician	laboratory technician	photographer	dietitian	medical technician	telephone operator
inspector/tester	optometrist	writer/editor	physical therapist	financial manager	payroll clerk
groundskeeper	technical writer	musician	radio/TV announcer	loan officer	accountant
mechanical engineer	veterinarian	wedding coordinator	counselor	insurance agent	dispatcher
driver	pharmacist	set designer	social worker	telemarketer	court reporter
	economist			travel agent	

Personality/Career Identification

Section One

Read the following lists of classes. Which list contains the classes you would be most interested in taking?

A	B	C	D
Technology Education	Physics	Art History	Sociology
Shop	Chemistry	Creative Writing	Psychology
Wood Working	Mathematics	Music	Interpersonal
Technical Drawing	Biology	Art	Communications
Auto Mechanics	Genetics	Interior Design	Human Relations
			Special Education
			Instruction Techniques

E	F
Business Management	Accounting
Leadership Course	Commercial Math
Starting Your Own	Record Keeping
Business	Business Law
Sales Strategies	Speed Reading
Networking	

Section Two

Read the following lists of occupations. Which list contains the occupations that you think would be most interesting.

A	B	C	D
ultrasound technologist	surgeon	fashion designer	athletic trainer
missile inspector	neurologist	editor	teacher
pilot	electrical engineer	cartoonist	library director
electronic repair person	food tester	cake decorator	detective
tree surgeon	pharmacist	photojournalist	career counselor
truck driver	veterinarian	public relations	personnel recruiter
		representative	

E	F
hotel manager	tax preparer
claims adjuster	telephone operator
landscape contractor	investment analyst
lobbyist	airline-radio operator
automobile sales person	medical record technician
sight seeing guide	proofreader

Section Three

In the list below circle the letter in front of any activity you think you would enjoy doing

A make a scale drawing	D work as a volunteer	C perform for others	D counsel people
C write a speech	F operate office	A fix a car	C arrange or compose
D teaching children	machines	E supervise work on a	music
E manage a sales	E attend a sales	project	B work in a science lab
campaign	conference	F take inventory	A operate motorized
B work with chemicals	A work outside	D meet an important	equipment
F check paperwork for	B work as a research	educator or therapist	
errors	assistant	F fill out forms	
C design furniture	B solve a technical	E run your own business	
	problem		

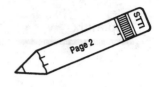

Personality/Career Identification

Which list of classes most appealed to you in Section One? _____

Which list of occupations appealed to you in Section Two? _____

Which letter did you circle most often in Section Three? _____

Based on this information determine your personality type(s) from the key below.

A = Technical/Realistic

B = Scientific/Investigative

C = Artistic

D = Social/Humanitarian

E = Business/Enterprising

F = Business Information/Conventional

Write down two occupation that you are interested in learning more about. You may select from the lists below or write down others you think of yourself.

1. _____

2. _____

A	B	C	D
Airplane Mechanic	Biologist	Poet	High School Teacher
Truck Driver	Medical Lab Technician	Musician	Marriage Counselor
Surveyor	Environmental Analyst	Journalist	Social Worker
Electrician	Writer of Scientific Articles	Composer	Speech Therapist
Farmer	Anthropologist	Actor/Actress	Juvenile Delinquency
Helicopter Pilot	Geologist	Artist	Expert
Machinist	Social Science Researcher	Singer	Substance Abuse
Welder	Astronomer	Entertainer	Counselor
		Novelist	Sociologist
			Rehabilitation Counselor

E	F
Advertising Executive	Certified Public Accountant
Real Estate Salesperson	Bank Teller
Small Business Owner	Computer Operator
Legislator	Credit Investigator
Business Executive	Inventory Controller
Reporter	Bookkeeper
Buyer	Auditor
Salesperson	Administrative Assistant

Suggestions for additional reading.

Bolles, R.N. (1994). *What color is your parachute? A practical manual for job hunters and career changers.* Berkeley, CA: Ten Speed Press.

Holland, J.L. (1992). *Making Vocational choices: A theory of vocational personalities and work environments.* Odessa, FL: Psychological Assessment Resources.

U.S. Department of Labor Bureau of Labor Statistics. (1992-1993). *Occupational outlook handbook.* Washington, DC: U.S. Government Printing Office. (This handbook is published every two years and is the best single source for information about occupations. See your counselor of library, or order from Superintendent of Documents, U.S. Government Printing Office, Washington, DC, 20402.)

CHECK LIST

At Home

_____ Dress neat, clean, and appropriately for the teaching assignment.

_____ Enter the school enthusiastic and serious about your role.

_____ If possible, arrive at the school at least 20 minutes prior to the beginning of classes.

_____ Be sure to take along your sense of humor, your **Super Sub Pack**, an objective for the day, two aspirin and a snack for yourself.

Prior to entering the class

_____ Report to the principal or the office to let them know you have arrived.

_____ Ask about the policies regarding students in the halls and student passes.

_____ Ask if there will be any special duties associated with the permanent teacher's assignment.

_____ Find out how to refer a student to the office.

_____ Look for the fire alarm and know the proper drill directions.

_____ Ask if there might be a student who has a medical problem.

_____ Obtain any keys that might be necessary.

_____ Find out how to report students who are tardy or absent.

_____ Find the locations of restrooms and the teacher's lounge.

_____ Ask the names of the teachers on both sides of your classroom and if possible, introduce yourself to them.

In the classroom

_____ If possible greet your students as they come in the door

_____ Enter the classroom with confidence, the first impression can take you a long way.

_____ If lesson plans are provided, follow them as closely as possible.

_____ If money needs to be collected, record the amount, the name of the student, and the purpose for the collection on a sheet of paper and turn it in to the office at the end of the school day.

_____ Locate the books, handouts, and papers that will be needed throughout the day.

_____ Study the seating chart or be prepared to make your own.

End of class

_____ If a teacher has classroom sets that are used by the students, be sure to have them all returned before anyone in the class leaves. It is easier to locate one book or calculator in a class of 30, than trying to find it in the whole school at the end of 7 periods.

_____ Remind students of homework. It is often helpful to write it on the board.

_____ Have students clean their desks and the area around their desk.

End of day

_____ Leave the desks, books, and classroom in good order.

_____ Turn in any money collected at the office.

_____ Fill out a "Substitute Teacher Report" and leave it with all other materials for the permanent teacher. A sample report form is located on page 200 of the appendix.

© Substitute Teacher Training Institute

Lesson and Activity Reference Guide

Substitute Teacher Professional Reference Guide

Mastering the Art of Substitute Teaching, S. Harold Collins 1979. ISBN 0-931993-02-4, Garlic Press, 100 Hillview Lane #2, Eugene, OR 97408, Phone (541) 345-0063 , Cost $8.95 + $3.00 S&H

Classroom Management for Substitute Teachers, S. Harold Collins 1982.

ISBN 0-931993-03-2, Garlic Press, 100 Hillview Lane #2, Eugene, OR 97408,

Phone (541) 345-0063 , Cost $7.95 + S&H (call for delivery cost to your area)

Instant Success for Classroom Teachers, New and Substitute Teachers, Barbara Cawthrone 1981. ISBN 0-9606666-0-5, Greenfield Publications, 8720 East Forrest Dr., Scottsdale, AZ 85256 , Phone (602) 994-1452, Cost $7.95 + $1.00 S&H

The First Days of School, How to be an Effective Teacher, Harry K. Wong & Rosemary Tripi Wong 1991. ISBN 0-9629360-06. Harry K. Wong Publications, 1030 W. Maude Ave. Ste 507, Sunnyvale, CA 94086, Phone (408) 732-1388, Fax (408) 732-2206, Cost: $24.95 + $4.25 S&H

Substitute Teaching - Tricks of the Trade. Randy Sturgeon 1994. LCN 94-75138. G&S Publishing. Send purchase requests to: Captured Moments, P.O. Box 2521, Lancaster, CA 93539-2521, Cost: $14.95 + $5.00 S&H. Make checks payable to "Captured Moments"

School Supply Companies

Delta Education 1-800-442-5444 to request a current catalog.

Hands-On Math activity books and supplies; Hands-On Science activity books and supplies

Nasco 1-800-558-9595 to request a current catalog.

Health, Arts & Crafts, Math, Science, Language Arts, Social Studies, & Music Materials

Books Available At Your Local Bookstore

The Mammoth Book of Fun and Games. Richard B. Manchester. ISBN 0-88486-044-2 ($12.95) Over 400 games, jokes, and puzzles.

The Giant Book of Games. Will Shortz. ISBN 0-8129-1951 ($15.00)

171 pages of games and puzzles compiled from Games magazine.

Brain Bafflers. Robert Steinwachs. ISBN 0-8069-8787-1 ($4.95)

96 pages of brain teasers.

Puzzles Perplexities & Obfuscations. George Hardy. ISBN 0-8069-8210-1 ($5.95)

96 pages of word puzzles and brain teasers.

More Two Minute Mysteries. Donald J. Sobol. ISBN 0-590-44788-2 ($2.95)

Over 60 mysteries to read and solve in two minutes or less.

More 5 Minute Mysteries. Ken Weber. ISBN 1-56138-058-X ($7.95)

34 mysteries to read and solve in five minutes or less.

© Substitute Teacher Training Institute

Journal of Lessons Taught

Date:	School:	Permanent Teacher:	Subject Taught
____	_____	_____	_____
____	_____	_____	_____
____	_____	_____	_____
____	_____	_____	_____
____	_____	_____	_____
____	_____	_____	_____
____	_____	_____	_____
____	_____	_____	_____
____	_____	_____	_____
____	_____	_____	_____
____	_____	_____	_____
____	_____	_____	_____
____	_____	_____	_____
____	_____	_____	_____
____	_____	_____	_____
____	_____	_____	_____
____	_____	_____	_____
____	_____	_____	_____
____	_____	_____	_____
____	_____	_____	_____
____	_____	_____	_____
____	_____	_____	_____

Substitute Teacher Report

To be left for the permanent teacher.

Substitute: _____   Date: _____

Phone Number: _____   Class: _____

Substituted for: _____   School: _____

Period	Notes about lessons	Notes about students
1		
2		
3		
4		
5		
6		
7		
8		

Messages for the permanent teacher:

I have some lesson ideas that I would like to teach in the areas listed. If you would like me to teach these just give me a call, and I will come prepared with these plans.

Please let me know some areas you feel I can improve, to be a better substitute for you.

Substitute Teacher Training Institute/Utah State University (800) 922-4693